PURPOSE AND MEANING OF LIFE A ISLAMIC PROSPECT

MUHAMMED HASHIM KUNNIL

BookLeaf Publishing

Presentation by BookLeaf Publishing
Web: www.bookleafpub.com
E-mail: info@bookleafpub.com

ISBN: 978-93-95890-57-1
First edition 2022

CHAPTERS

CHAPTER-1

WHO IS HUMAN BEING

WE HUMANS ARE BIOLOGICALLY AN ANIMAL AND SPIRITUALLY A SUPERIOR LIVING ORGANISM. OUR MIND IS THE CONSCIOUSNESS SPACE THAT POSSESS THE KNOWLEDGE WHO WE ARE.SO WE ARE A ORGANISM OF BODY, SOUL AND MIND LIVING ON THE EARTH.

OUR FOREFATHERS ARE ALSO HUMANS THEY BORN AS HUMAN AND LIVED AS HUMAN. YES, I KNOW SOME SCIENTIST HAS A DIFFERENT VIEW, SOME BELIEVES OUR GENERATIONS STARTED FROM A SINGLE CELL LIVING ORGANISM AND THROUGH GENERATIONS OF EVOLUTION DIFFERENT SPECIESES EVOLVED DUE TO NATURAL SELECTION, AMONGST FROM THAT SPECIESES WE HUMANS ARE ONE.

I AM ACTUALLY APPRECIATING THEIR LEVEL OF IMAGINATION BUT NOT AGREEING IT AS REALITY. I AM ALSO AGREEING WITH EVOLUTION THEORY IN SOME OF THEIR POINTS. I WILL DISCUSSED IT IN A LATER CHAPTER

AS PER ISLAM ALLAH THE ALMIGHTY GOD IS THE ONLY CREATORE AND SUPREAM SUSTAINER OF THE UNIVERSES. EVERY CREATION IS DONE BY HIM. I AM TELLING ABOUT THE CREATION NOT TRANSFORMATION OF SOMETHING. ALLAH ALMIGHTY CREATED ALL OF US FROM NOTHING AND

ALLAH GIVE EXISTENCE TO US AND HE IS THE ONLY MASTER APROVER OF OUR DESTINY

ISLAM REMEMBERING THAT ALLAH IS INFINITE IN ALL MEANS AND WE ARE   LIMITED IN ALL MEANS.

ALLAH CREATE THE FIRST HUMAN MEN ADAM AND FIRST LADY HAWWA AT THE HEAVEN WHICH SITUATED IN BETWEEN OUR RESIDING ARSH – UNIVERSE AREA. ADAM CREATED AROUND 150 THOUSAND YEARS BEFORE. BEFORE ADAM ALSO EARTH CONTAINED HUMAIN LIKE CREATURES BUT THEIR SOUL IS ENTIRELY DIFFERENT FROM NEWLY CREATED ADAM AND HAWWA. OUR SOUL GIVES SUPREAMACY TO THE HUMAN RACE OVER OTHER ANIMALS.

THE EARLY LIVED HUMAN BODY ANIMALS ARE ACTUALLY NOT REAL HUMANS BECAUSE THEY ARE HUMAN BY BODY BUT NOT BY SOUL. THEIR SOUL IS A COMPARATIVELY LOW QUALITY ONE AND MORE RELATED TO OTHER ANIMALS. THEY ARE VERY FIGHTING NATURE ANIMALS OF THAT TIME. THEIR SOME GENERATIONS LIVED AT THE SAME TIME OF ADAMS SOME GENERATIONS BUT BOTH ARE NOT MIX-UP OR CROSS BREED.AFTER ADAMS SOME GENERATIONS ALLAH ALMIGHTY END THEIR GENERATION AND MAKE EARTH SAFE FOR ADAMS GENERATIONS.

WE CAN GET SOME KNOWLEDGE ABOUT THEM IN QURAN ALSO. WHEN ALLAH PLANNED THE ADAMS CREATION GOD ALMIGHTY DISCUSSED IT WITH ANGELS(MALAK). ANGELS SUDDENLY REPLAYED THAT OH GOD ALMIGHTY ARE YOU PLANING TO MAKE WAR MONGING ANIMALS. WE ALL KNOW ANGELS NOT KNOWN THE UP COMING FUTURE. ONLY ALLAH KNOWNS THAT. THEN HOW THEY GET THIS INFORMATION, BECAUSE THEY BEFORE SEENED ALLAH EXPLAINED KIND OF BODY ANIMALS ON EARTH AND MOST OF THEM ARE ALL TIME FIGHTING LIVING CREATURES.

QURAN AGAIN EXPLAINS HOW ALLAH CHANGED THIS VIEW OF ANGELS(MALAK) BY MAKE ADAM WITH REAL HUMAN SOUL AND CONDUCT A EXAMINATION INFRONT OF THEM. ADAM PASSED THE EXAM SUCCESSFULLY WITH HIS INDIVITUAL GOD GIVEN EBILITY. THEN ALLAH SAID ALL THE ANGELS TO SUJUDH(RESPECT) HIM. ANGELS ARE DID THE SUJUDH (RESPECT) BUT THEIR TEACHER EBLISE A HIGHER QUALITY JINN (A KIND OF CREATION FROM FIRE) NOT DONE. BECAUSE HE BELIVE THAT HE IS SUPERIOR THAN ADAM BECAUSE HIS BODY MADE FROM FIRE AND ADAMS FROM MUD, HE DID NOT UNDERSTANT SOUL MAKES THE DIFFERENCE. ALLAH REMOVED HIM FROM HIS POSITION BECAUSE OF HIS

LESS KNOWLEDGE, JELOUSY AND PRIDE. HE REQUISTED SOME FAVOURES FROM ALLAH, GOD ALMIGTY ALLOW SOME OF THEM. FROM THAT TIME EBLIS BECOME THE FIRST AND GREATER ENEMY OF MANKIND. THAT EBLIS IS BECOME SHAIYTHAN(DEVIL) BY HATEFULLNESS TO ADAM AND ADAMS GENERATIONS. EBLIS TAKE PERMISSION FROM ALLAH FOR HIS EXISTENCE UP TO QIYAMATH DAY (HUMAN BEINGS LAST DAY ON EARTH) AND INTERACTION AND COMMUNICATION EBILITY WITH ADAMS AND ADAMS GENERATIONS. HE ALSO TAKE PERMISSION FOR BRINGING OTHER JINNS TO HIS PATH. ALLAH ALOWED THAT ALSO. SO EBLIS AND HIS COMPANIAN JINS ARE COLLECTIEVELY CALLED AS SHAIYTHAN.

SO THE POINT IS OTHER HUMAN APPEARED ANIMALS ARE ALSO LIVED BEFORE FIRST REAL HUMAN ADAM. THE PRIMARY IDENTITY OF A HUMANS ARE HIS OR HER SOUL. THAT POSSESS 60% OF HIS/HER EARTHLY IDENTITY BY CONTROLING CAPACITY THE REMAINING 40% IS POSSESSED BY HIS OR HER BODY. MIND IS THE PORTION OF COMBINATION OF A PORTION OF BOTH SOUL AND BODY. MINDS CONCIOUSNESS AND CONTROLING CAPABILITIES HANDLING 30 TO 40 PERCENTAGE OF OUR TOTAL

CONTROLING SYSTEM, THE PERCENTAGE RANGE IS BECAUSE IT VARY PERSON BY PERSON.

OUR BODY IS COME THROUGH THE LINKAGE OF OUR ANCESTRIAL GENERATIONS, BUT OUR SOUL DID NOT COME THROUGH GENERATIONS. OUR SOUL DID NOT HAVE ANY FOREFATHERS AND IT WILL NEVER PRODUCE ANY BIOLOGICAL ANCESTERS, BUT IT CAN MAKE US AS A PERSON OF INSPIRATION FOR GENERATIONS. BODYS PHYSICAL AND BIOLOGYCAL PERFORMANCE AND SOULS INNER PERFORMANCE MAKE EACH OF US A UNIQ PERSON.OUR CHILD WILL GET OUR BODY ANCESTRIALSHIP BUT OUR CHILD WILL NEVER GET OUR SOUL ANCESTRIALSHIP, SAME TIME OUR CHILD AND SURROUNDING PEOPLES MAY GET OUR SOULS CULTURE.

EACH HUMANS SOUL IS DIFFERENT FROM ONE ANOTHER AND THE RANGE OF DIFFERENCE IS MORE COMPARED TO BODY BECAUSE SOUL IS THE BIGGER IDENTITY. AFTER DEATH ALSO SOUL WILL CONTINUE TO LIVE WITHOUT BODY, BUT BODY WILL NEVER LIVE WITHOUT SOUL, THAT IS WHY I AM INTERESTED TO CALL SOUL IS THE PRIMARY IDENTITY OF HUMAN BEING. I WILL TELL ONE MORE THING THE BODY-SOUL COMBINATION IS THE SPECIALITY OF LIVING ORGANISMS IN THIS UNIVERSE. IN OTHER ARSH-UNIVERSES THE SYSTEM WILL VARY. ALLAH

ALMIGHTY DON'T HAVE SUCH KIND OF SEPARATION, IF ALLAH WISHES SOME STYLE ALLAH WILL ACT IN THAT STYLE.

AS PER MY OBSERVATION AND KNOWLEDGE HUMAN BEING HAVE DIFFERENT QUALITY OF SOUL. I CATEGORIZED SOUL QUALITY IN A GRADE SYSTEM. I WILL GIVE A BRIEF EXPLANATION.

I AM REPRESENTING SOUL QUALITY IN 1 TO 10 GRADE SYSTEM

1 –MEANS INEFFICIENT

5- ENERGETIC AND CREATIVE

AND

10-MEANS MOST SUPREME QUALITY

MOST OF THE PEOPLES SOUL QUALITY IS RANGING BETWEEN 1 TO 6 AND 5 TO 10 CONSIDERED AS SUPERIOR SOULS. IT IS POSSIBLE TO UP-LIFT OUR SOUL QUALITY BY OUR SELF BUT NOT DIRECTLY, WE CAN MAKE IT SHARP AND MORE SYCRONISABLE TO THE EXTERNAL WORLD. SOULS UPGRADATION AND DOWN GRADATION IS FULLY DIRECTLY BELONGS TO ALLAH ALMIGHTY, ALLAH DOING THE UPGRADATION AND DOWNGRADATION ACCORDING TO HIS WILL. IN THIS MATTER OUR PRAYERS MAY

MAKE GOOD CHANGES, OUR GOOD ACT TO PEOPLES AND SOCIETYS MAKE CHANGES, OUR SELF PURIFICATION AND STAY AWAY FROM BAD WAYS WILL MAKE CHANGES.

NORMALLY ALLAH ALMIGHTY EQUALLY DISTRIBUTING DIFFERENT QUALITY SOULS IN DIFFERENT ETHNIC SOCITIESE. IN SOME CENTURIES ALLAH DISTRIBUTE IT IN SOME DIFFERENCES BECAUSE OF ALLAHS PRE –WRITTEN PLANING OF SOME MISSIONS. BUT IF WE LIVE IN GOOD LIFE WAY CHANCES OF GETTING UPGRADED IS POSSIBLE AT ANY TIME.

AS LIKE SOUL OUR BODY ALSO HAVE DIFFERENT NATURE AND CAPABILITIES. I CATEGORIZED IT IN POINT SYSTEM, IT IS IN 1 TO 20 RANGE

1- LESS ACTIVE BODY

5- ACTIVE BODY

10- ATHLETIC BODY

15- ATHLETIC AND BEAUTIFUL-HANDSOME BODY

20- BEAUTIFUL-HANDSOME AND HEALTHY BODY.

THE SOUL AND BODY COMBINATION IS DIFFERENT FOR PERSON BY PERSON. SOME PERSON POSSESSES A SOUL GRADE OF 7 AND BODY OF12, SOME POSSESS SOUL GRADE OF 4 AND BODY OF 15, SOME POSSESS

SOUL GRADE OF 8 AND BODY OF 18. THE COMBINATION IS RELATED TO PERSON AND NOT DIRECTLY RELATED TO ANY ETHNICITIES. ALL ETHNIC SOCIETIES HAVE DIFFERENT TYPE OF BODY-SOUL COMBINATIONS.

WE CAN MAKE IMPROVEMENTS IN OUR BODY ALSO, IN BODY SUBJECT WE HAVE MORE DIRECT IMPROVEMENT CONTROL WITH OUR SELF. WE CAN UPGRADE OUR SOUL AS THROUGH I PRE EXPLAINED WAY. THE COMBINATION OF BODY AND SOUL IMOROVEMENT WILL RESULT IN THE TOTAL IMPROVEMENT OF OUR MIND.

EATING GOOD FOOD, GOOD SLEEPING HABITS, EXERSISE, DRINKING SUFFICIENT WATER, ETC WILL IMPROVE YOUR HEALTH AND BODY CONDITIONS.

MEDITATION, TENSION SURVIVING PRACTICES, GOOD LIFE CONTROL AND HABITS WILL BOOST YOUR MIND DEVELOPMENT DIRECTLY.

SUBMITTING YOUR WILL TO GOD ALMIGHTY, GOOD MORALS, GOOD VALUES, ETC WILL HELP YOU TO GETTING SOUL UPGRADATION

THE ORGANS MOSTLY RELATED TO OUR MIND FROM BODY SIDE ARE BRAIN, HEART, LUNGS AND DIGESION ABSORBTION ORGANS.

INTERACTION AND COMMUNICATION ZONE BETWEEN THESE ORGANS AND OUR SOUL IS

CONSIDERING AS MIND. THESE INTERACTION MOSTLY HAPPENS THROUGH OUR NERVE SYSTEM. SOUL IS THE ADMINISTRATOR OF THESE COMMUNICATION PATH, COMMUNICATION, ADOPTATION AND ACCEPTING ARE HAPPENS IN BOTH SIDE.

AS A RELIGIOUS MEANING SOME PERSONS BODY POSSESS GOOD MORAL STATE AND SOME PERSONS SOUL POSSESS GOOD MORAL STATE.

SAME TIME FEW PERSONS BOTH POSSESS BAD OR GOOD STATE. SO THIS ALSO MAKE DIFFERENCES IN PERSONS BEHAVIOUR AND CHARACTER.

HUMAN IDENTITY SYMBOLIC DIAGRAM

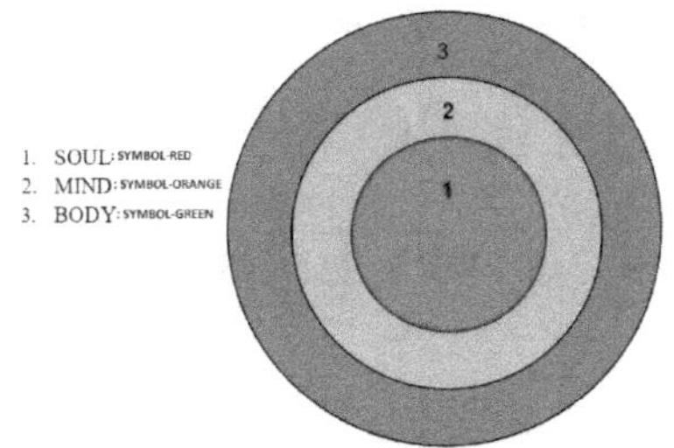

1. SOUL: SYMBOL-RED
2. MIND: SYMBOL-ORANGE
3. BODY: SYMBOL-GREEN

CHAPTER 1: DIAGRAM 1

CHAPTER-2

12

IS ANY CREATOR OR MASTER POWER OF THE UNIVERSES?

WE HUMAN BEINGS HAVE DIFFERENT OPINIONS ABOUT CREATOR AND SUSTAINER OF THE UNIVERSES. I AM CONSIDERING THE VIEWS OF FIVE WORLD KNOWN RELIGIONS WHICH I UNDERSTOOD THAT THEIR BEGINNING FROM GOD ALMIGHTY'S INFLUENCE.

HINDUISM, JUDAISM, BUDDHISM, CHRISTIANITY AND ISLAM HAVE DIFFERENT VIEW POINT ABOUT CREATOR OF EVERYTHING AND MASTER POWER, I WILL HAVE INTERESTED TO CALL ANOTHER NAME GOD ALMIGHTY

FIRSTLY, I WILL HAVE DISCUSSED ABOUT THE HINDU RELIGION THE SANADHAN DHARMA VIEWPOINT ABOUT THE GOD ALMIGHTY VEDHIC RELIGION OR SANADHANA DHARMA SANADHAN DHARMA FOLLOWERS HAVE DIFFERENT UNDERSTANDING IN THE SUBJECT OF GOD. CURRENT DAY BASIC FORM IS TEMPLE PRACTICES AND WORSHIP OF DIFFERENT GODS AND GODDESS IN THE FORM OF IDLE WORSHIP AND RITUALS. SANADHANA MEANS CONSTANT OR NON-CHANGEABLE KNOWLEDGE AND PRACTICES. ACTUALLY THAT WORD IS THE CORE OF ALL RELIGIOUS PRACTICES AND KNOWLEDGE OF ALL RELIGIONS

AS PER HISTORICAL EVIDENCE SANADHAN DHARMA'S GRASS ROOT IS BASED ON THE ANCIENT MESOPOTAMIAN CIVILIZATION. I

AM CONSIDERING IT AS A RELIGION OF ABRAHAMIC (IBRAHIMIYA) FAMILY. THE PRIMARY PARTICIPANTS OF SANADHAN DHARMA ARE KNOWN AS BRAHMINS, MEANS PEOPLE OF ABRAHAM(IBRAHIM).

PROPHET ABRAHAM IS BORN IN MESOPOTAMIA, PRESENT DAY IRAQ 5000 YEARS BEFORE. HE IS CONSIDERING AS THE ONE OF THE GREAT PROPHET AND FATHER OF MODERN ADAMIC RELIGIONS JUDAISM, CHRISTIANITY AND ISLAM.

MOST OF THE PEOPLES KNOWN THE HISTORY OF PROPHET ABRAHAMS BOTH SON IZHAQ, ISMAIL AND THEIR GENERATIONS, BUT MOST OF US DIDN'T KNOW THE HISTORY OF HIS FIRST FOLLOWER FROM HIS MOSEPOTOMIAN LIFE. THAT PEOPLES ARE THE FIRST GENERATION OF BRAHMIN SOCIETY. NOW A DAYS INDIAN BASED BRAHMINS ARE ONLY KEEPING THAT NAME. MOST OF THE OTHER BRAHMIN SOCIETY'S TRANSFORM TO ISLAM AFTER PROPHET MUHAMMAD.

AT TIME OF BRAHMIN SOCIETY'S FORMATION IN MESOPOTAMIA THEY FACE SO MANY RELIGIOUS PROSECUTIONS BECAUSE THEY ARE BELIEVING IN A RELIGION OF ONLY ONE ALMIGHTY GOD. THIS KIND OF HARSH SITUATIONS LEADS THEM TO START HIJRA (MIGRATION) TO ANOTHER PLACES OF THE WORLD. THEY SEPARATE AS DIFFERENT GROUPS AND

START THE JOURNEY OF MIGRATION. MOST OF THEM MOVED EAST AND NORTH WORDS AND THEY SETTLED IN SURROUNDING SUCH PLACES. WEST WARDS MOVEMENT HAPPENED VERY LESS BECAUSE OF THE PRESENTS OF ASSYRIAN (LATER THIS NAME IS USED BY INDIAN BRAHMINS TO CALL INDIAN DRAVIDAS AS AZURAS) COMMUNITY'S IN THERE. ASSYRIANS ARE AN ETHNICITY WITH THEIR OWN RELIGION AT THAT TIME. BRAHMINS ARE MOSTLY ARISES FROM THE ARYAN COMMUNITY OF MOSEPOTOMIA. BEFORE PROPHET ABRAHAM (IBRAHIM) ALSO AN ARYAN -ASSYRIAN CLASH HISTORY IS THERE IN MESOPOTAMIA. ALL ARYANS OF MESOPOTAMIA DID NOT BECOME BRAHMINS. THE REMAINING ARYAN PORTION ALSO OPPOSE THE NEWLY BRAHMIN BECOME ARYANS.

AROUND 4000 YEARS BEFORE BRAHMINS COMMUNITY CROSESS THE SINDU RIVER AND ENTER THE PRECENT DAY INDIAN LAND. THAT TIME INDIAN RULERS ARE DRAVIDIANS WHO ARE RATIONALIST PEOPLES OF THAT TIME. DRAVIDIAN PEOPLES FIRST BIG CULTURAL CENTERS ARE SITUATED IN HARAPPA AND MOHAN JADHARO PRESENT DAY PAKISTAN SAME TIME THEY HAVE SMALL SETTLEMENT IN DIFFERENT ASIAN REGIONS.

DRAVIDIAN RULERES WELCOMED THE BRAHMIN COMMUNITY AND GIVE SPECIAL STATUS. THEY PROVIDE FREE LAND FOR THEIR SETTLEMENT. BRAHMINS PRACTICED THEIR RELIGION AS LIKE THEY BEFORE. RULERS IMPRESSED IN THEIR NATURE OF WORSHIP AND MORALS. THEY POSTED THEM IN HIGHER POSITIONS OF THEIR ADMINISTRATION SYSTEM OF THE KINGDOMS. FROM THAT TIME THE MODERN HISTORY OF INDIAN CONTINENT BEGIS.

AS STATED BEFORE BRAHMINS RELIGIOUS PRACTICES STARTS FROM MONOTHEISTIC RELIGIOUS STYLE BUT IT GO THROUGH SEVERAL CHANGES THROUGH CENTURIES AND BECOME A RELIGIONS BELIEF SYSTEM OF GOD AND SEVERAL DEVANS(POWERS). THIS NEW CHANGES ALL HAPPENED JUST BEFORE THEY ENTER INDIA.

THIS TRANSFORMATION TREND IN THE BRAHMINS RELIGION THEN CONTINUOUS TO SEVERAL THOUSAND YEARS THAT IS MODERN HISTORY OF SANADANADHARMA. NEW RELIGIOUS SCRIPTURES AND TEXTS WRITING BEGINS AND CONTINOUING.IN PORTION OF PERIOD OF THIS TIME A NEW TREND STARTED, SOME GREAT SCHOLORS OF THAT TIME THINK THAT IT IS ESSENTIAL TO WRITE TEXT BOOK WITH SOME SELF CONTRIBUTION AND INTERPRETATION. THE RESULT OF THE TREND IS WE HUMANS GET LOT OF GREAT BOOKS OF KNOWLEDGE, AS

THE SAME TIME SO MANY BOOKS CHANGED THE OLD TRADITION OF BELIEFE AND UNDERSTANDINGS OF BRAHMINS RELIGION. THAT TIME BRAHMANISM BECOME RELIGION OF MOST OF THE CONDINENT AS A RELIGION OF MULTIPLE GOD AND GODESSESS.

THIS TYPE OF CHANGES MAKE SOME PROBLEMS WITH THE RELIGION ALSO. THE HINDU RELIGION LOST ITS UNITENESS IN SCRIPTURE AS WELL AS PRACTICE. THIS HAPPENED BETWEEN B.C 1500 AND B.C 500.

THAT TIME A NEW CHANGE ALSO HAPPENED IN INDIAN SUBCONDINENT. THAT IS THE INTRODUCTION OF BUDHISM. BUDHIST MISSIONARY ACTIVITYS GET VERY POPULARITY IN THAT TIME, THIS NEW SITUATION MAKE A BIG CHANGE IN THAT TIMES HINDU PEOPLE. LOT OF PEOPLE CONVERTED TO BUDHISM. FROM THIS POINT WE CAN CONSIDER AS THE STARTING OF MODERN HINDUISM THE SANADHANADARMA

INTER-RELIGIOUS DIOALOGS AND DEBATED STARTED BETWEEN BOTH HINDU SCHOLERS AND BUDHIST MONKS. AFTER A.D 500 HINDU SCOLERS AND MONKS STARTED TO CONCENTRATE ON THE RELIGIOUS RENAISENCE. BUT THEY SADLY UNDERSTOOD THAT IT IS NOT POSSIBLE THROUGH THE DIRECT TEACHING AND PRACTICING OF THE RELIGIOUS

SCRIPTURES AND TEXTS. BECAUSE LOT OF THEM BECOME CONTRADICTORY THROUGH THE BEFORE ACTIVITIESE AND SOME ARE NOT FROM SOURCE OF RELIGION.

IN THIS CRITICAL SITUATION THEY WISELY ADOPT THE METHOD OF PHYLOSOPHYCAL APPROACH. ACTUALY THAT IS THE ONLY POSSIBLE WAY THEY HAVE.

GREAT PHILOSOPHERS LIKE SANKARACHARYA, RAMANUCHARYA, MADHVACHARYA ARE EMERGES IN THIS TIME. MOST OF THEM ARE LIVED BETWEEN A.D 7TH AND 12TH CENTURY.

SHANKACHARYAS DEVOLEPED VERSION OF BHADHARAYANS ADWAIDA PHYLOSOPHY GET FAST REACH IN A VERY SHORT TIME. IN TAMILNADU SRIRAMANUCHARYAS VISHISHTADWAITHA GET MORE REACH. I WILL GIVE BRIEF DETAILS AT THE END OF THIS SECTION. MANGLOORE BASED MADHWACHARYA IS ALSO A RENOWED FIGURE HIS BRANCH OF PHYLOSOPHY CALLED AS DWAITHAVEDANTHA. OTHER THAN MAJOR THREE VIEW POINTS SO MEANY OTHER VERSIONS ARE ALSO WRITTEN ON THAT TIME BUT NOT GET THIS MUCH ATTRACTION FROM RELIGIOUS SCHOLERS AND BELIVERS.

SAME TIME NORTH INDIAN REGIONS A NEW TREND OF SUFI-BHAKTHI PRASTHANS EMERGES. THEY ALSO RECEIVED THE GENERATIONS. PERSONALITIES LIKE

SOORDAS, KABIR DAS, MEERA BHAI ARE WELL ACCEPTED.

NOW I WILL BRIEFLY DISCUSS ABOUT THE BELIEF SYSTEM

THE MOST COMMON PRACTICE ARE NOW A DAYS TEMPLE PRACTICES AND RITUALS. THAT ARE MOSTLY RELATED TO IDLE WORSHIP

NOW I WILL DISCUSS ABOUT THE PHYLOSOPHYCAL SIDE

ADWAITHA

AS PER ADWAITHA ONLY BRAHMA (UNIVERSAL SOUL) IS PERMANENTLY EXISTING. JAGATH (WORLD) IS MAYA (ILLUSION). EACH THINGS CONTAINS BOTH BRAHMA AND JAGATH INCLUDING US. BUT ONLY BRAHMA IS CONSTANT. ABOUT JAGATH AWAITHIS ARE HAVE SO MEANY VIEW POINTS. THE MAIN THREE ARE

1) IT IS A ILLUSION BRAHMAM SATHYAM JAGATH MIDHYA AS PER MY UNDERSTANDING THIS VIEW POINT IS NOT OKAY

2) IT IS CHANGEABLE LIKE A MUD USING FOR POTERY

3) THE MODERN DAY VIEW OF SOME ADWAITHIS

   ONLY BRAHMA THAT IS JAGATH

THEY ARE ADOPTING ATOMIC PHYSICS FOR EXPLAINING THIS VIEW

ATOMS MEANS ELECTRONS, PROTONS AND NUTRONS ALL ARE PLASMA STATE, SO EVERY THING BUILD UP OF SAME MATERIAL THAT IS COLLECTIEVELY CALLED BRAHMA IN THE FORM OF JAGATH.

I WILL GIVE A POEM OF ADWAITHA STYLE

"BRAHMA U ARE THE EARTH U ARE THE SKY U ARE THE SUN U ARE THE MOON U ARE ME U ARE THEY U ARE THE STONE U ARE THE SOIL ONLY U…. ONLY U…. ONLY U…. U ARE THE BORN U ARE THE UNBORN…. WE ALL ARE BRAHMA NOTHING OTHER THAN BRAHMA."

NOW A DAYS MOST OF THE HINDU SHRINES FOLLOWING ADWAITHA PHYLOSOPHY. SOME FOLLOWING VISHISHTADWAITHA AND RARELY DWAITHAVEDANTHA.
VISHISHTADWAITHA
VISHISHTADWAITHA PHYLOSOPHY IS DEVELOPED BY RAMANUCHARYA. I PERSONALLY MOST INTERESTED IN THIS PHYLOSOPHY AMONGS HINDU PHYLOSOPHYS.
IT IS ALSO BELIEVING IN BRAHMA THE UNIVERSAL SOUL AND ADWAITHA. BUT A DIFFERENCE BRAHMA HAS TWO PARTS ONE IS GOD ANOTHER IS JAGATH. RAMANUCHAARYA INTERESTED TO CALL GOD AS VISHNU. GOD HAVE INFINITE

POWER AND WE HAVE LIMITED. THAT IS THE CORE OF VISHISTADWAITHA.

AT THE BEGINNING TIME AWAIDIS NOT PARTICIPATED IN THE TEMPLE ACTIVITIES THIS LEADS THE HINDU PEOPLES LESS GOD FEARING. AS PER AWAITHIS UNDERSTANDING EVERY THING CONTAINS BRAHMA THEN WHAT IS THE NEED OF PRAYERS AND SPECIAL TREATMENTS. THAT CONDITION LEADS TO THE DEVELOPMENT OF VISISHTADWAITHAM THE RELIGIOUS PHYLOSOPHY LATER ADWAIDIS ALSO STARTED THE BRAHMA WORSHIP.

DWAITHA VEDANTA

DWAITHA VEDANTA INTERPRETATION IS THE MOST TRADITIONAL STYLE. IT DIRECTLY DEALING WITH MOST OF THE PART OF THE HINDU SCRIPTURES. ACTUALLY MOST OF THE PART OF THE SCRIPTURE SUPPORTING THIS INTERPRETATION.

ITS UNDERSTANDING IS VERY SIMPLE GOD IS DIFFERENT WE ARE DIFFERENT. WE CAN CONSIDER IT AS THE ORTHODOX INTERPRETATION OF HINDU SCRIPTURES.

DWAITHA VEDHANDIST ALSO HAVE DIFFERENT VIEWS ABOUT GOD AND JAGATH.

ABOUT GOD IS SOME BELIEVES IN SINGLE GOD AND SOME IN MULTIPLE GODS ABOUT JAGATH (WORLD INCLUDING US) IS SOME

BELIEVES GOD ACT ONLY THROUGH OUTSIDE WORLD

SOME BELIEVES GOD ACT THROUGH BOTH INSIDE AND OUTSIDE

MOST OF THESE PHYLOSOPHYS BUT DO NOT GIVES CLEAR UNDERSTANDING ABOUT BRAHMAS OR GODS CREATOR ROLE. MOST UNDERSTANDING ARE RELATED TO SUSTAINER OR MAINTAINER PARTS.

JUDAISM

JUDAISM IS ONE OF THE GREAT ABRAHAMIC RELIGION. IT ORIGINATED IN THE LAND OF PALASTINE AND ISRAYEL.ABRAHAM IS CONSIDERED AS THE FOREFATHER OF ABRAHAMIC(IBRAHIMIYATH) RELIGIONS LIKE JUDAISM, CHRISTIANITY, ISLAM AND BRAHMANISM.

JUDAISM, CHRISTIANITY AND ISLAM CONSIDERING ABRAHAM AS ONE OF THE GREAT ENLIGHTED PROPHET AND MESSENGER OF GOD ALMIGHTY. HE BORN AT UR A MESAPOTEMIAN CITY SITUATED IN PRECENT DAY IRAQ AROUND 3000 B.C.

AT FIRST SECTION OF THIS CHAPTER WE DISCUSSED PROPHET ABRAHAMS MESEPOTAMIAN MISSION. AFTER SUCCESS OF HIS MISSION GOD ALMIGHTY SEND HIM TO LAND OF PALESTIN AND THEN FOR A SHORT TIME TO ARABIA. HE SPEND MOST OF HIS LIFE IN THIS THREE AREAS.

JUDAISM IS A RELIGIOUS COMMUNITY AS WELL AS A MIXTURE OF SOME ETHINC COMMUNITYS STARTED THROUGH ABRAHAMS SON IZHAQ AND HIS PALESTNIAN SOCIETY. ETHNICALLY PROPHET ABRAHAM IS A ARYAN AND HIS FIRST WIFE ZARA IS A ASYRYAN THEIR FIRST SON IS PROPHET IZHAQ. ABRAHAM MARRIED TWISE, AT THE TIME OF IZHAQS BIRTH ABRAHAM WAS IN ARABIAN TRAVEL

WITH HIS SECOND WIFE HAJIRA. AMONGS HIS TWO SONS HE FIRST SAW HIS SECOND SON ISMAYIL AND YEARS LATER HE MET IZHAQ.

GENERATION OF ISMAYIL AND OTHER MESEPOTAMIAN ARYAN AND ASYRYAN SOCIETYS MIXED UP AND FORM THE MODERN ARAB SOCIETY. THROUGH IZHAQ AND ISMAIL PHROPHET ABRAHAM HAVE DIRECT BIOLOGYCAL CONNECTION WITH THESE SOCIETYS.

JUDAIC COMMUNITY HAVE A HISTORY OF MORE THAN 4500 YEARS, BUT DUE TO STRICT ETHINIC POLICY THE RELIGION NOT SPRED MORE TO OTHER ETHNIC PEOPLES. THEY PRACTICED THEIR RELIGION INSIDE THEIR COMMUNITY ONLY.

AFTER ABRAHAM PROPHET MOSES IS CONSIDERED AS THE KEY MESSENGER OF GOD YAHOWA THE ALMIGHTY. JUISH COMMUNITY HAVE A LONG HISTORY OF SETTLEMENT AND RESETTLEMENT. THE FIRST SETTLEMENT HAPPENED IN THE TIME OF PROPHET JOSEPH(YUSUF) AT EGYPT AND RE-SETTLEMENT HAPPENED TO PALESTINE-ISRAYEL IN THE TIME OF PHAROVAS OF EGYPT AND PROPHET MOSES.

PROPHET MOSES IS CONSIDERING AS THE FATHER OF MODERN JUDAISM. AMONGS ALL PROPHETS, AT EARTH PROPHET MOSES HAS EXPERIENCED THE LIVE PRECENCE OF YAHOWAS HOLLY SPIRIT (AS PER QURAN

ALLAHS ALMIGHTYS HOLLY SOUL) THE GOD ALMIGHTYS NATURE INSIDE THIS UNIVERSE. THE OTHER HUMAN EXPERIENCED SUCH PRECENCE IS MARRY THE MOTHER OF PROPHET JESUS THE NASRETH ACCORDING TO QURAAN.

AS PER ADAMIC RELIGIONS UNDERSTANDING PROPHETS ARE GETTING ALMIGHTY GODS MESSAGES AND REVELATIONS THROUGH DIFFERENT WAYS. THE FOLLOWING ARE THE WAYS GOD ALMIGHTY USING.

THROUGH DIRECT EXPERIENCE: PROPHET MUHAMMED EXPERIENCED NEAR ARSH (A HOLLOW GLOBE BARRIER BETWEEN GOD ALMIGHTY AND THIS UNIVERSE, HEAVEN AND HELL. GOD ALMIGHTY IS OUTSIDE THE ARSH. INSIDE THE ARSH GOD ALMIGHTY ACTING AS HOLLY SOUL)

PROPHET MOSES SEEN ALLAH ALMIGHTY HOLLY SOUL AT SINAI MOUNTAN

2) THROUGH ANGELS(MALAK): PROPHET MUHAMMED AND PROPHET JESUS GET SOME OF THEIRE REVELATION THROUGH THIS WAY

3) THROUGH DREAM WITH SPIRITUAL AFFIRMATION FROM GOD: THIS WAY PROPHET ABRAHAM(IBRAHIM) IS THE MOST

PROMINET FIGURE ANOTHER IS PROPHET JOSEPH(YUSUF)

4)DIRECT COMMUNICATION BETWEEN PROPHETS ROOH AND ALLAH ALMIGHTY HOLLY SOUL THIS IS THE MOST COMMON WAY GOD ALMIGHTY DEALING WITH EACH PERSON ESPECIALY PROPHETS. THE DIFFERENCE IS THE PERSENTAGE OF CONNECTION BETWEEN PROPHET AND HOLLY SPIRIT IS MUCH HIGHER THAL COMMEN MAN. ANOTHER THING IS PROPHETS ARE ALWAYS AWARE AND BECOME CONCIOUS IN THIS COMMUNICATION PATH.

THIS ARE THE FOUR METHODS GOD ALMIGHTY USESING TO REVEAL HIS MESSAGE TO HIS MESSENGERS OF MANKIND.

AMONGS THIS FOUR METHODS PROPHET MOSESS EXPERIENCED THREE, THAT IS WHY HE IS CONSIDERED AS ONE OF THE GREAT PROPHET OF ALL TIME.

PROPHET MOSES(MOOSA) IS CONSIDERED AS THE SAVIOUR OF JEWISH COMMUNITY FROM THE BAD ACTS AND PROSECUTIONS OF THAT TIMES PHAROVAS OF EGYPT.

HIS MISSION IS FIRSTLY CONCENTRATE ON THE TRANSFORMATION OF PHAROVAN RULE TO A BETTER ONE FOR EVERY ONE. AFTER LOT OF YEARS MISSION, HE DID NOT SUCCEDED IN IT. PHAROVA BECOME MORE AND MORE RUDE TO JEWISH COMMUNITY

AS LIKE BEFORE. THIS EGYPTIAN LIFE UNITE THE JEWISH COMMUNITY ON ETHINIC BASE.

EGYPTIANS ARE ETHNICALY ARYAN -AFRO -GREECK MIXED ETHINIC PEOPLES. SO MORE THAN RELIGION THE ISSUE WAS AN ETHNIC ISSUE.

AS PER YAHOWAS HOLLYSPIRITS DIRECTION PROPHET MOSES PLANNED A HIJRA (SAFE TRANSFER TO AN ANOTHER LAND) OF HIS JEWISH COMMUNITY TO THEIR FOREFATHERS LAND PALASTINE-ISRAYEL. THROUGH THIS ACTION JEWISH COMMUNITY GET THE REAL FREEDOM AFTER CENTURYS. THEY CROSS THE SEA AND REACH SUCCESFULLY TO NEAR THEIR LAND WITH YAHOWAS SPECIAL HELP. SAME TIME THE PHAROVEN ARMY FOLLOWED THEM FOR KILLING BUT THEY DID NOT SUCCEEDED IN THE MISSION AND LOT OF THEM DIED IN THEIR ALSO.

THIS INSIDENT IS CONSIDERED AS A MILESTONE IN JEWISH HISTORY. WHEN REACH NEAR SINAI MOSES BECOME ALONE AND PRAYED WITH YAHOWA AFTER SOME DAYS HE RETURE BACK TO HIS SOCIETY. THEIR HE SEEN AN ENTIRELY DIFFERENT SITUATIONS.

I AM USING QURANIC EXPLAINATION ABOUT THIS INSIDENT. THIS INSIDENT ALSO GIVES A SOLUTION FOR ENTIRE HUMAN KIND. THAT IS NO NEED TO KILL A

RELIGIOUS BLASPHEY PERSON AND OPPOSSER OFF RELIGIOUS TRUTHS. JUST CONSIDER IT AS A HUMAN ACT LEAVE IT, BUT ALSO NO NEED TO KEEP THAT MAN IN THE SAME COMMUNITY AS A BELIEVER OF THAT COMMUNITY OR WELL WISHER OF THAT COMMUNITY. SAME TIME DO NOT MAKE ANY KIND OF DISTURBENCE IN HIS OR HER LIFE IN THIS MATTER.

AS PER QURAN AND JEWISH HISTORY THE PERSON IS SABIRI HE IS ALSO JEW AND A BELIVER BEFORE. HE IS ACTUALY A PROMINENT PERSON OF THE COMMUNITY. AT EGYPTIAN LIFE ALSO HE WORKED FOR PHAROVA IN GOOD POSITIONS. WHEN MOSESS WENT FOR PRAYER HE STARTED TO LEAD THE COMMUNITY HE INTRODUCED SOME NEW RELIGIOUS RITUALS LIKE MAKE A IDLE OF COW AND LEAD THE COMMUNITY TO ITS WORSHIP. THESE ARE HAPPENED JUST WITH IN ONE WEAK AFTER PROPHET MOSES WENT TO PRAYER.

THIS IS HAPPENED BECAUSE OF JEWS ARE NOT SO REFRESHED RELIOUSLY.THEY DON NOT GET SO MUCH FREEDOM IN EGYPT BEFORE I EXPLAINED. BECAUSE OF THAT ISSUE PROPHET MOSESS DID NOT GET ENOUGH FREEDOM TO TEACH THE RELIGIOUS TRUTHS AND PRACTICES TO THEM. THE OLD STYLE OF RELIOUS PRACTICES ARE ALSO BECOME CORRUPTED.

AFTER PRAYER TO YAHOWA MOSES PLANNED TO START THE RELIGIOUS TEACHING TO THE COMMUNITY. IN THIS SITUATION SABIRYS INTEREPTION AND DISTERBENSES HE IDENTIFIED, ACTUALY THE COMMUNITY IS TOTALLY FOLLOING PROPHET MOSES BUT THEY MIS GUIDED BY SABIRY. WITH FULL POWER AND COMMUNITY LEADERSHIP IN HIS HAND PROPHET MOSES RELEASE THE SABIRI FREE, AND TELL THEM TO GO SOME OTHER PLACE OR TO ANOTHER COMMUNITY.ACTUALY THIS IS A WIN-WIN SITUATION OF HUMAN KIND. BASICALY WE ALL ARE HUMAN IF SOME ONE HAVE DIFFERENT UNDERSTANDING AND BELIEFE THEY CAN FOLLOW THEIRE WAY.THEY CAN ALSO TEACH THAT WAY TO COMMUNITY IF THEY WANT, COMMUNITY IS NOT PRIVET PROPERTY, WITH OUT COMMUNITYS SUPPORT WE CAN NOT BAN A PERSON.

ACTUALY LATER JEWISH SCHOLERS ALSO PRACTICED THIS STYLE AT SOME LEVEL. AS PER MY UNDERSTANDING AT THE TIME OF JESUS(EESA) THE NASRATH THEY ARE ON WRONG SIDE WITH GOOD PROCEDURE UP TO SOME LEVEL BUT IN THE END THEIR PROCEDURE ALSO BECOME WRONG. I AM TELLING THE SUBJECT OF PROPHET JESUS THE NASRETH. WITH GREATER POLITYCAL POWER COMPERED TO JESUS THEY SPEND YEARS FOR MAKING THE SOCIETYS

OPINION AGAINST HIM. ONES A BIGGER PORTION COMES WITH THEIR SIDE THEY STARTED THE PROCECUTION STAGE. BUT DEATH PENALTY DECISION FOR RELIGIOUS MATTER IS AGAINST PROPHET MOSESS PRACTISES. SO THEY VIOLATE THE RELIGIOUS RULE.

AFTER PROPHET MOSES LOT OF OTHER PROPHETS ARE ALSO COME TO JEWISH COMMUNITY. JEWISH COMMUNITY SETTLED IN ISRAYEL-PALASTINE AND FLOURISHED AS A RICH CULTURE.

JEWISH PEOPLES BELIEVES YAHOWA THE ALMIGHTY GOD AS THE CREATOR, SUSTAINER AND ALL POWER ONE GOD OF THE ENTIRE UNIVERSE. THEY ACTUALY NOT SO AWARE ABOUT THE HOLLY SPIRIT PART OF YAHOWA THEIR UNDERSTANDING IS GOD ACT EVERY WHERE IN A UNIQ STYLE.

BUDHISM

BUDHISM IS CONSIDERED AS A RELIGION OF RATIONALISM. BUDHIST RATIONALISM MOSTLY IN ITS THEORY AND IN SOME PPRACTICES BUT RITUALS IN NOW A DAYS NOT A RATIONAL ONE BY ITS STYLE.

IT HAS LOT OF BELIEVES SYSTEM AND RITUAL PRACTICES THAT ARE NOT IN THE RELIGION AT THE TIME OF ITS BEGINNING.

I CONSIDERING SREE BUDHA AS ONE OF THE MIGHTIGHTYEST MESENGER OF GOD ALMIGHTY LIVE ON THE EARTH. GOD ALMIGHTY GIVE HIM THE RATIONAL STYLE APROCH OF MISSION TO THE SOCIETY. THAT IS A SECRET OF GOD ALMIGHTYS ACTION. GOD GIVES DIRECTION OF DIFFERENT STYLE APROCH TO THE PROPHETS. SOME MESENGERS ADOPTED THE CREATIVE WAY AND SOME IN THE LOGIC WAY. PROPHET SREE BUDHA DIRECTED TO ADOPT THE PURE LOGIC WAY. THAT IS THE WISE CHOICE ACCORNING TO THAT GENERATION CONDITIONS.

SREE BUDHA DID NOT DENIED THE PRECENCE OF GOD ALMIGHTY BUT ALSO HE DID NOT TELL ABOUT GOD TO THE PEOPLE. THIS BECAUSE OF THAT TIMES INDIAN SOCIETYS RELIGIOUS CONDITIONS. THAT TIME INDIAN SOCIETY IS UNDER THE HARSH STAGE OF CAST SYSTEM AND DISCRIMINATION BASED ON ETHNIC CAST

THROUGH THE RELIGIOUS THOUGHTS AND PRACTICES.

PROPHET SREE BUDHA BORN AT PADALI PUTHRA PRECENT DAY INDIA. WHEN HE REACHED HIS ENLIGHTMENT STAGE THROUGH SOUL (ROOH) RELATION TO GOD ALMIGHTY HE STARTED TO PREACH THE RELIGION. THIS STAGE OF NEW WISDOM IS CALLED BY BUDHIST AS ENLIGHTMENT.

HE STARTED TO ADVOCATE AND SPREAD HIS THOUGHTS TO SURROUNDING AREAS OF HIS LAND. HE REJECTED THE IDEA OF CAST SUPREMACY AND PREACH PEACE AND COEXISTENCE. THIS IS THE PRIME REASON OF HIS ACCEPTANCE TO THAT TIMES INDIAN SOCIETY.

IT MAKE A THOUGHT REVOLUTION IN INDIAN SOCIETY AT THE SAME TIME PROPHET BUDHA FOCUSED ON THE INDIVITUAL ENLIGHTMENT OF EACH PERSON THROUGH HIS WAY OF PRACTICE. HE SAID TO THE SOCIETY YOU BECOME YOUR ON LIGHT AND YOUR ON SUN TO THE LIFE PATH. DON'T FOCUS ON OUT SIDE SPIRITUAL UPLIFTING YOU ARE SUFFICIENT FOR YOUR OWN ENLIGHTMENT. SO MEDITATION IS STARTED TO PRACTICE AS A WAY OF PERSONAL ENLIGHTMENT.

PROPHET BUDHA IS NOT TOO MUCH SAID ABOUT THE HUMAN SOUL IN HIS TEACHINGS HIS TEACHINGS ARE MOSTLY RELATED TO HUMAN BODY AND MIND.

THAT TIME THE VEDIC RELIGIOUS PRACTISNERS MOSTLY CONCENTRATED ON THE BODY INTERPRETION OF HUMAN IDENTITY AND CAST SYSTEM BASED ON THAT.

FOR OUT STRECHING BUDHISM VADIC FOLLOWERS LATER MORE CONCENTRATE ON THE SOUL INTERPRETATION OF HUMANS THAT REDUCE THE HARSHNESS OF CAST SYSTEM IN INDIAN SOCIETY. SHANKARACHARYA THE GREAT INDIAN PHYLOSOPHER GIVE MORE BOOST TO SOUL INTERPRATION OF EVERYTHING. THAT IS A UPGRADATION OF PROPHET SREE BUDHAS TEACHING FROM MIND LEVEL IDENTITY OF HUMAN. THAT IS WHY SANKARACHARYA IS CALLED AS PRASHCHANNA (NON-VISIBLE BUDHA) BUDHA BY SOME VEDIC SCHOLERS. THIS POSITIVE INTERPRETATION APPROCHES FROM HINDU SCHOLERS AND MONKS AGAIN GIVE THEM A SUCCESS IN INDIAN SOCIETY. PROPHET SREEDUDHA IS THE DIRECT REASON BEHIND THIS CHANGE. BUT LATER MOST OF THE BUDHIST LOST THE IDEA ABOUT THE REALITY OF THE MINDS KNOWLEDGE AND THEY STARTED TO CONCENTRATE ON THE BODY INTERPRETATION OF HUMAN IDENTITY THAT LEADS TO THE LESS POPULARITY OF BUDHISM IN INDIA. SO THIS INTERPRETATION INTER CHANGES MAKE

THE SUCCESS DIFFERENCE BETWEEN VEDIC
RELIGION AND BUDHISM IN INDIA.

34

CHRISTIANITY

WE ALL KNOWS CHRISTIANITY IS THE MOST POPULAR RELIGION OF PRECENT TIME. IT HAS RELATION WITH JEWISH COMMUNITY ALSO. ACTUALY CHRISTIANITY IS A NEXT STAGE EXTENSION OF JUDAISM. IT IS STARTED FROM PROPHET JESUS THE NASRETH AS PER CHRISTIAN UNDERSTANDING JESUS CRIST THE ONE PART OF HOLLY TRINITY OF GOD ALMIGHTY.

JESUS (EESA) BORN IN JEWISH COMMUNITY OF PALASTINE-ISRAYEL THROUGH GOD ALMIGHTYS SPECIAL ACTION FROM THE WRITTEN DESTINY OPTIONS. JESUS DO NOT HAVE BIOLOGICAL FATHER, HE HAVE ONLY MOTHER. FROM THIS POINT LOT OF PEOPLE BELIEVES HE IS THE SON OF GOD. REALITY IS HE IS THE ONE OF THE ALL TIME GREAT PROPHET OF HUMAN KIND. BUT THAT IS NOT RELATED TO HIS BIRTH. FIRST MAN ADAM IS A PROPHET BY MISSION AND DO NOT HAVE BOTH FATHER AND MOTHER. FOR ADAMS CREATION GOD ALMIGHTY USED ONE METHOD, FOR HAWWAS(EVE) GOD ALMIGHTY USED ANOTHER METHOD FOR OUR CREATION GOD ALMIGHTY USING GENERAL METHOD SAME AS FOR JESUS CREATION GOD ALMIGHTY USED AN ANOTHER METHOD. WE KNOW EVERYTHING IS POSSIBLE FOR GOD, IF GOD WANTS.

ISLAM CONSIDERING PROPHET JESUS AS ONE OF THE TOP FIVE PROPHETS. AROUND 600 TO 700 PROPHETS PARTICIPATED IN THE GOD ALMIGHTYS MISSION FROM LAST 150 THOUSAND YEARS OF ENTIRE HUMAN HISTORY. PROPHET NOHA, ABRAHAM, MOSES, JESUS AND MUHAMMAD ARE THE PROMINENT FIGURES AS PER ABRAHAMIC TRADITION PROPHET SRE BUDHA AND PROPHET LUKMAN ARE OTHER GREAT PROPHETS. PROPHET DULKERNAIN IS THE UP COMING ONE.

AS PER CHRISTIAN UNDERSTANDING THEY BELIEVING GOD ALMIGHTY HAVE THREE FORM OR THREE STATES AT THE SAME TIME. ONE IS FATHER STATE OR FORM, OTHER HOLLYSPIRIT STATE OR FORM AND JESUS HUMAN STATE OR SPIRITUAL FORM.

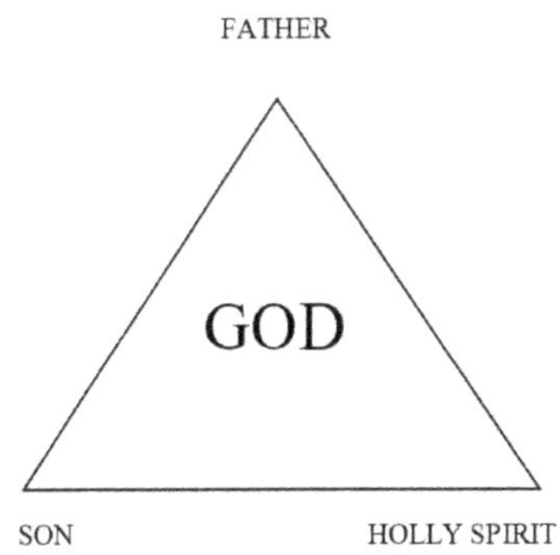

CHAPTER 2: DIAGRAM 1

DIFFERENT VIEWS ARE ALSO AVAILABLE ABOUT THE STATE, RATIO AND POWER.
MY ADAMIC (GOD ALMITYS FIRST TO LAST MISSIONS IDEOLOGY) RELIGIOUS VIEW POINT IS GOD ACT IN DIFFERENT STYLE ONE OF HIS STYLE IS HOLLY SOUL OF GOD ALMIGTY. BUT JESUS IS NOT A PART OF GOD, HE IS A HUMAN AND ONE OF THE GREATEST PROPHET OF ALL TIME. JESUS NEVER CLAIM HE HAS A PART OF GOD, LATER CENTURYS OF CHRISTIANITY

CHANGED HIS STATUS FROM PROPHET TO
PART OF ALMIGHTY GOD. THAT IS THE
REALITY.
AS PER CHRISTIANITY GOD ALMIGHTY IS
THE CREATOR, SUSTAINER AND AL POWER
GOD OF THE ENTIRE UNIVERSE.

ISLAM
ARSH AND UNIVERSES SYSTEM
CROSS-SECTION DIAGRAM.

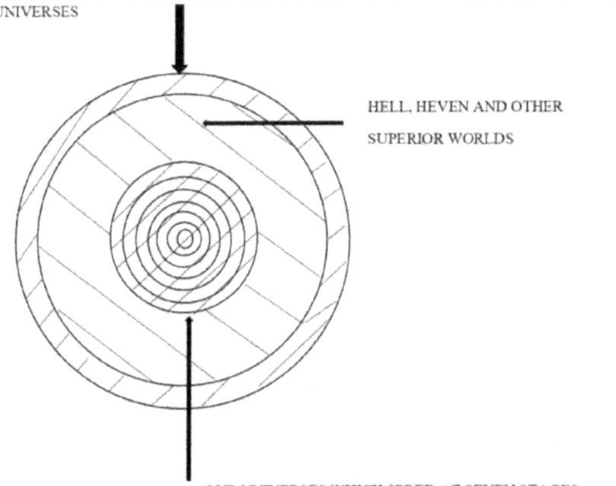

OR IN QURAANIC WORD SEVEN SKYS, AS PER QURAAN OUR NEAR BY SKY IS THE SKY OF STARS, WHICH IS TERMED AS FIRST SKY. IN THIS IMAGE OUR EARTH SITUATED SKY IS AT THE INSIDE FIRST SKY OF UNIVERSES.

OUT SIDE ARSH ALLAH ALMIGHTY AT INFINIT POWER AND INFINITITY WITH OTHER ARSH-UNIVERSES SYSTEMS

INSIDE ARSH ALLAH ALMIGHTY PRECENT IN THE FORM OF HOLLY SOUL

CHAPTER-2 DIAGRAM-2

ARSH: A HOLLOW GLOBE BARRIER BETWEEN ALLAH AND THIS UNIVERSE OUT SIDE ARSH ALLAH AT INFINIT POWER AND OTHER ARSH –UNIVERSES HEAVEN, HELL AND OTHER AREAS: SITUATED INSIDE THE ARSH BETWEEN ARSH AND OUR UNIVERSE

OUR UNIVERSE: SITUATED INSIDE THE ARSH NEXT TO HEAVEN AND HELL. IT HAVE SEVEN PORTIONS ALLAH LIKE TO CALL AS SEVEN SKYS. AT THE FIRST SKY PORTION OUR GALAXYS SITUATED. UNIVESE INCLUDES ALL LIVING AND NON LIVING THINGS INCLUDING US
HOLLY SOUL OF ALLAH: THE GENERAL STYLE OR WAY OF ALLAHS INTERACTION WITH THIS UNIVERSE

HOLLY SOUL OF ALLAH NOT PERMANENTLY STAYING IN A POSITION OR IN SIDE THE ARSH. AS PER QURAN ALLAHS HOLLY SOUL SOME TIMES PASSES THROUH OUR FIRST SKY PORTION OF UNIVESE ALSO.
ALLAH ALMIGHTY MADE SO MEANY ARSH-UNIVERSE SYSTEMS OTHER THAN OUR ARSH-UNIVERSE.THAT ALL CREATIONS MAKE ALLAH ALMIGHTY ACTIVE AND HELPING TO ACT MORE CREATIVE.
BEFORE THE CREATION OF ARSH-UNIVERSE MODEL ALLAH IMPLIMENT AND PRACTICE AN OPEN MODEL ALLAH AND CREATIONS RELATION. ALLAH KEEP HIS STATUS AS THIN AND ALLOW HIS CREATIONS TO LIVE WITH IN HIS SURROUNDINGS. BILLIONS OF YEARS PASSESS THIS SYSTEM STARTED TO BECOME PROBLEM FOR ALLAH.SOME INTELIGENT CREATIONS STARTED TO FIND ALLAHS SOME SECRETS BECAUSE OF THE FREEDOM ALLAH GIVEN. SOME OF THEM

ARE STARTED TO MIS USE SUCH KNOWLEDGES. THEN ALLAH END THAT ERA AND CREATE THE NEW SYSTEM OF ARSH AND UNIVERSE.

EACH ARSH AND UNIVERSES ARE DIFFERENT IN ALL MEANS ONLY SOME STRUCTURAL SIMILARITYS.

AS PER ISLAMIC UNDERSTANDING ALLAH ALMIGHTY IS THE ONLY CREATOR, SUSTAINER AND ALL POWER GOD OF ALL HIS CREATIONS. ALLAH ALMIGHTY EXISTING IN INFINITY AND HOLDS INFINITE POWER. CREATURES ARE FROM THE DIRECT REDUCTION OF ALLAHS REALITY THROUGH SINGLE OR DIFFERENT STAGES WITH ALLAH ALMIGHTYS WILL, AND ALLAH ALMIGHTY GIVEN SEPERATE IDENTITY FOR EACH CREATIONS. THE FIRST STAGE OF REDUCTION FROM ALLAH ALMIGHTY IS EMTYNESS. THEN ALLAH ALMIGHTY CREATED AND THEN TRANSFORMED EVERYTHING FROM EMPTYNESS.

THE CREATIONS WITH SOUL POSSESS A FREEDOM OF ACT UNDER DIFFERENT NATURAL LAWS AND LIVING ENVIRONMENT IMPLIMENTED BY ALLAH ALMIGHTY AND REMAINING CREATIONS CONTINOUES UNDER DIFFERENT NATURAL LAWS AND ENVIRONMENT IMPLEMENTED BY ALLAH ALMIGHTY.

CHAPTER-3

DESTINY-QADHR

MOST OF THE WORLD RELIGIONS BELIEVES IN THE DESTINY OF GOD BUT IN DIFFERENT FORMS. IN SOME SOCIETYS ASTROLOGY IS A BRANCH OF THEIR RELIGIOUS LIFE BECAUSE IT CLAIMS THAT IT IS THE WAY TO READ ONE PERSONS PRE-WRITTEND DESTINY.

IN SOME SOCIETYS FORCASTERS FROM RELIGIOUS SIDE DOING THIS ACTIVITY. THE MOTTO OF ALL THESE ACTIVITIESE IS TO READ THE PRE-WRITTEN DESTINY AND IF POSSIBLE DO SOME RITUALS TO MAKE IT GOOD FOR THE PERSON.

I CAN SURELY DENAY ASTROLOGY WAYS POSSIBILITY TO READ THE DESTINY BUT MY BELIEVING IN PRE-WRITTEN DESTINY, LIVE-DESTNY AND FINAL DESTINY IS A NON-CHANGABLE ONE. MOST SUCCESS FULL WAY OF FORECATING IN NOW A DAYS SCIENTIFIC FORCASTING. EXAMPLE FOR THAT IS WHETHER FORCASTING IT HAVE AN ACCURACY OF 50%. BUT IN SOME SOCIETIESE RELIGIOUS PERSONS NOT ADOPTING THIS METHODOLOGY OF FORECATING THEY STILL FOLLOWING LESS ACCURATE OLD PRACTICES. I AM TELLING THAT WE CAN PREDICT A FUTURE THING OR INSIDENT OF OUR INDIVITUALS OR SOCITYS BY CALCULATING THE KNOWLEDGE SURROUNDED THE PERSON OR SOCIETY BUT WE CAN NOT READ THE PRE-WRITTEN DESTINY OF A PERSON.

AS PER ISLAM ALLAH KNOWS EVERYTHING BEFORE IT HAPPENEDS. HOW IT POSSIBLE WE MAY THINK, BECAUSE ALLAH THE ALMIGHTY GOD CREATED THE WORLD INCLUDING US THROUGH DIFFERENT STAGES. BEFORE EACH STAGES OF CREATION ALLAH PREPARED THE WORKING SOFTWARE AND HARDWARE PROGRAM AND DESIGN, IT IS CALLED AS PRE-WRITTEN DESTINY OR THE FIRST STAGE OF DESTINY (QADHR). BEFORE FIRST MODERN HUMAN ADAMS CREATION ALLAH PREPARED ADAMS ENTIRE GENERATIONS PRE-WRITTEN DESTINY RELATED TO THEIR LIFE WITH DIFFERENT CHOICES AND OPTIONS IN EACH STAGES OF ENTIRE LIFE OF A PERSON. INCLUDING ENTIRE OPTIONS OF EACH SITUATION ALLAH KNOWS ALL THE POSSIBILITIESE, LOWER AND UPPER RANGE OF EACH PERSON LIFE. THE FIRST REASON FOR MADE THE PRE-WRITTEN OR PRE-PROGRAMMED DESTINY IS TIMELY COMPLETION OF THE TOTAL PLAN OF GOD ALMIGHTY. THE SECOND IS, IT IS THE PATH OF CHOICES AND OPTIONS OF LIFE WHEN CREATION HAPPENS AND IT IS THE RANGE OF APPROVALS GOD ALMIGHTY WISHED TO GIVE. BUT ALL THESE ARE HIDED FROM US, SO NO NEED TO REED IT. BUT WE CAN TRY TO PREDICT OUR FUTURE BY SCIENTIFIC WAY PREDICTION, SAME TIME NOT CONSIDERING THAT AS THE 100% REALITY.

I WILL GIVE AN EXAMPLE OF SCIENTIFIC PREDICTION, WE CAN EXAMIN OUR ENTIRE BODY WITH MOST ADVANCED MEDICAL EXAMINATION AND IDENTIFY FUTURE CHANCES OF DESISES AND HEATH CONDITIONS WITH SOME MORE CLARITY, AT THE SAME TIME WE ARE UNABLE TO FIND OUR DEATH BY GETTING KILLED OR ACCIDENTS. SO 100% PREDICTION IS ALSO NOT POSSIBLE IN ALL MEANS.

NOW I WILL DISCUSSE ABOUT THE SECOND STAGE OF DESTINY THAT IS LIVE-DESTINY. THIS IS ACTIVATED AFTER CREATION. AT EACH SITUATION AND EACH STAGE OF LIFE WE WILL GET LOT OF CHOICES AND OPTIONS BECAUSE OUR PRE-WRITTEN DESTINY IS PREPARED BY ICLUDING LOT OF CHOICES AND OPTIONS AT EACH SITUATION OF LIFE. AMOMGS FROM SUCH CHOICES AND OPTIONS WE WILL SELECT OR UNDEGONE THROUH SOME SMALL NUMBER OF CHOICES AND OPTIONS IN EACH SITUATION.THIS HAPPENED THROUGH OUR ACTION & REACTION, SOCIETYS ACTION & REACTION, INVOLMENT OF OTHER LIVING AND NON-LIVING THINGS AND FIRSTLY& FINALY GOD ALMIGHTYS APPROVAL OVER THE BEGINNING AND THROUGH ALL THE STAGES OF CHOICES ESTABLISHMENT LIVELY. I AM TELLING THAT EACH AND EVERY TIME GOD HAVE LIVE RELATION WITH THIS WORLD. NORMALY AROUND TOTAL 20% OPTIONS

ARE STRICTLY INSISTING BY GOD ALMIGHTY IN DIFFERENT STAGES OF OUR LIFE. THE REMAINING SITUATIONS OF EACH STAGES OF A PESONS LIFE GONE THROUGH THE UNIVERSAL AUTOMATED SYSTEM OF LIFE UNDER THE OPTIONS IN THE PRE-WRITTEN DESTINY WITH GOD ALMIGHTYS APPROVAL, GOD ALMIGHTYS STRICT INVOLVEMENT MEANS GOD ALMIGHTY STRICTLY INSISTING OUR 20% OPTIONS AND CHOICES AS PER GOD ALMIGHTYS WILL. THIS 20% IS SPREAD IN THE WHOLE 100% OF THE PERSON'S DESTINY. AS WITH THE REMAINING 80% MOST OF THEM ARE NOT FIXED IN ANY SPECIFIC CHOICES. THAT WILL BE ACTIVATED AS PER THE LIVE SITUATION AND CONDION WITH ALLAH ALMIGHTYS APPROVAL.

I WILL GIVE AN EXAMPLE OF WORKING PRINCIPLE OF LIVE-DESTINY BASED ON THE PRE-WRITTEN DESTINY. IF WE ARE ON TRAVEL AND WANT VEHICLES FOR THAT. SUPPOSE WE ARE USING OUR PRIVET VEHICLE WE HAVE MORE CONTROL AND DISICION POWER ON IT. SO CHANCES TO MAINTAIN CONTROL ON THAT OPTION IS MORE. I PREVIOUSLY SAID ALLAH ALMIGHTY ALLOWS AND APPROVES MOST OF OUR PREFERED OPTIONS WITH NUTRAL STAND IF WE WISHES, THEN GETTING THAT IS MORE RELATED TO SURROUNDING SITUATION AND OUR ACTIONS. IF WE USE

PUBLIC VEHICLES THE CHANCES TO GET AND MAINTAIN IS BECOME LITTLE BIT COMPETATIVE BECAUSE OTHER PUBLICS ARE ALSO DEPENDING THAT VEHICLES. I AM TELLING THAT OUR PRE-WRITTEN DESTINYS ARE INDIVITUAL BASED SAME TIME MUTUALY LINKED ALSO, MUTUAL SITUATIONS ALSO EVERYWHERE. ALLAH HAVE THE MASTER COPY AND CONTROL OVER ALL THE DESTINY OF THE UNIVERSES. SUPPOSE WE ENTER IN A BUS THERE ARE 20 SEAT VACANT. THAT MEANS WE HAVE A CHOISE OF 20 SEAT OPTIONS WITH STANDING OPTION ALSO. IF SOME OTHER PERSONS ENTERED IN BUS AT SUCH SITUATION THAT MEANS OUR DESTINY HAVE LINK WITH THEM ALSO. I PREVIOUSLY SAID ALLAH IS THE EXAMINER AND MOST OF THE TIME ALLAH DID NOT STRICTLY PLACING US IN ANY OPTION OF A SITUATION OR STAGE OF OUR PRE-WRITTEN DESTINY. I ALSO SAID THAT EVERY SITUATION AND STAGES WE HAVE LOT OF CHOICES AND OPTIONS BUT IN REAL LIFE WE UNDERGOSE ONLY THROUGH SOME CHOICES AND OPTION BECAUSE THAT IS THE POSSIBILITY RANGE. I WILL GIVE AN EXAMPLE SUPPOSE AT A TIME MULTIPLE CHOICES AND OPTIONS LIKE WALKING, TAKING, HEARING MUSIC ETC, ARE WE SELECTED FROM DIFFERENT OPTIONS OF OUR PRE-WRITTEN DESTINY AT THE SAME ACTIVITY TIME MAY BE ANOTHER OPTION

OF SLEEPING ETC, ARE ON OUR PRE-WRITTEN DESTINY, THAT MAY BE NOT POSSIBLE AT THAT TIME. OUR PRE-WRITTEN DESTINYS SOME PORTIONS BECOME OUR LIFE BY ALLAHS MASTER APPROVAL CONTROL. APPROVAL ON LIVE-DESTINY. AROUND 80% TIME ALLAH APROVES THE OPTIONS FROM THE RESULT OF SITUATIONS AND STAGES, ALLAH STRICTLY APROVES AS PER ALLAHS INTEREST IS NORMALY 20% OF A PERSONS LIVE-DESTINY AMONGS FROM THE OPTION OF ALLAHS PRE-WRITTEN DESTINY. WE UNDERGOES THROUGH SOME CHOICES AND OPTIONS FROM ALL CHOICES AND OPTIONS OF OUR PRE-WRITTEN DESTINY BY THE RESULT OF OUR CONTRIBUTION, OUT SIDE WORLD CONTRIBUTION AND ALLAHS DECISION OR FINAL APROVAL.THIS IS CALLED OUR LIVE DESTINY OR OUR EARTHLY LIFE.

IN SOME AREAS QURAN ALLAH ALMIGHTY INFORM US THAT ACT OF OUR HANDS MAKE ALL PROBLEMS ON EARTH AND SEA. THESE WORDS INDICATES THE ACTION POWER OF HUMANS, THIS IS THE ACTION STAGE OF LIVE-DESTINY THROUGH THE OPTIONS OF PRE-WRITTEN DESTINY. IN SOME AREAS OF QURAN ALLAH ALMIGHTY INFORM US THAT NOTHING WILL HAPPENDS IN EARTH AND SKY WITH OUT ALLAHS KNOWLEDGE. IN SOME AREAS ALLAH INFORMING US THAT NO ONE CAN DO ANY THING EVERYTHING IS

HAPPENDS AS PER ALLAHS WISH. THIS INFORMATIONS IS RELATED TO THE MASTER CONTROL AND APROVAL POWER OF ALLAH ALMIGHTY ON LIVE-DESTINY AS PER THE CHOICES AND OPTIONS OF OUR PRE-WRITTEN DESTINY. ALLAH ALMIGHTYS WISH AND METHOD OF APPROVAL IS I EXPLAINED BEFORE, ALLAH CAN INTERMIT IN OUR LIFE AT ANY STAGE AND ANY TIME.

BEFORE FINAL DESTINY I WILL TELL ABOUT THE SABR AND SHUKR. IN OUR LIFE WE SHOULD ALWAYS PRACTICE SABR (FORGIVENESS AND PROGRESSIVE ACTION) AND SHUKR (THANKFULNESS TO GOD ALMIGHTY) FOR PEACE, SUCCESS AND GOD ALMIGHTYS ISHQ (LOVE).

NOW I WILL EXPLAIN FINAL DESTINY OR FINAL QADHR. ALLAH WILL COMPLETE THE QADHR BY APPLY IT AFTER KIYAMATH DAY THE LAST DAY OF HUMANS ON THE EARTH. THIS WILL HAPPENS IN FINAL JUDJMENT DAY OR FAINAL DESTINY DAY AT MAHSHARA A SPECIAL PLACE FOR THE JUDGEMENT.

AFTER OUR DEATH AT EARTH OUR SOUL WILL GO TO GOD ALMIGHTYS CUSTODY IN A SPECIAL PLACE. OUR BODY BECOME DEAD AND OUR SOUL CONTINOUES LIFE. AT THE END OF KIYAMATH DAY NO HUMAIN WILL REMAIN AS LIVE IN THEIR BODY AT EARTH. THAT TIME ALLAH WILL REGENERATE EACH HUMANS BODY AND ALLOW EACH SOUL TO

RE-ENTER IN IT AGAIN. WE WILL GET LIFE AGAIN IN OUR BODY AT A FIXED AGE OF 33 YEARS.

IN JUDGEMENT DAY ALLAHS HOLLY SOUL WILL ACT AS JUDGE AND PROPHETS OF EACH GENERATION WILL ACT AS THE SHAFA'ATH AUTHORITY (REFERENCER) OF THEIR GOOD PEOPLES. PROPHETS GET WHOLE KNOWLEDGE ABOUT THEIR GENERATION BY ALLAHS SPECIAL ENLIGHTMENT TO THEM AT THAT TIME. THEIR GENERATIONS EACH PERSONS GOOD AND BAD BOOK PREPARED BY THE ANGELS(MALAK) WILL COLLECTIEVELY ENLIGHTING TO THE PROPHETS MIND.

AS PER THAT KNOWLEDGE PROPHETS CAN REFER A AVERAGE OR GOOD PERSON FOR JANNAH THE HEAVEN. ALLAH WILL NEVER REJECT SUCH REFERENCES BECAUSE PROPHETS WILL NEVER REFER A BAD PERSON AND ALLAH KNOWS EVERYTHING.

SOME LONG GENERATIONS OF SOME SOCIETYS MAY NOT HAVE PROPHETS SUCH SITUATIONS ARE ALSO NORMAL IN SUCH SITUATIONS ALSO NORMAL PROCEDURE ALLAH WILL MAKE THE FINAL DECISION.

THIS IS THE THIRD PART OF OUR DESTINY(QADHR), THE FINAL DESTINY.

AT THE TIME OF JUDGEMENT DAY EACH HUMANS GET THEIR GOOD AND BAD BOOK WRITTEN BY ANGELS(MALAK) WILL BE ENLIGHTED TO THEIR MIND WITH IN

SECONDS. THAT TIME EVERY HUMANS REMAINS THEIR EVERY PART OF LIFE EVEN FORGETED THINGS. THEN ALLAH ASKS TO US ABOUT OUR LIFE AND ACTIONS. WHO SUCCEDED IN THAT STAGE IS SUCCEDED IN THE LIFE. WHO WILL FAIL IN SUCH STAGE MOSTLY FAILED IN THE LIFE.

THESE ARE THE DECIDING FACTORS OF JUDGEMENT DAYS WIN OR LOSE
TRUE UNDERSTANDING OF ALLAH GOD ALMIGHT AS HUMAM POSSIBLE MANNER AND SUBMIT OUR WILL TO HIM
PRACTICE JUSTICE IN EACH LIFE SITUATIONS
GOOD ACTIONS
AWAY FROM BAD ACTIONS

I KNOW MOST OF THE HUMANS LIVING PRECENT DAY NOT WELL AWARE ABOUT ALLAH ALMIGHTY IN TRUE UNDESTANDING, IS ANY PROBLEM FOR THAT? THAT IS DEPENDS UP ON YOU, BUT I AM SURE YOU ARE OKAY AT THE REMAINING THINGS AND YOU DID NOT MUCH AWARE ABOUT ALLAH BECAUSE OF YOU DID NOT EXPOSURE TO SUCH KNOWLEDGE YOU HAVE CHANCE. ONLY KAFIRS AND MUNAFIQS AND BAD PEOPLES HAVE PROBLEM WITH ALL THESE THINGS.

I WILL EXPLAIN WHO IS KAFIR, HE OR SHE IS A PERSON WHO REALLY UNDERSTANT THE THRUTH OF ALLAH AND ISLAM BUT NOT ACCEPTING IT OR ACT AGAINST IT BECAUSE OF EARTHLY BENEFITS. ALL NON-MUSLIMS ARE NOT KAFIRS. WHO IS MUNAFIQ, HE OR SHE IS A PERSON WHO REALLY NOT UNDERTAND OR BELIEVED IN ALLAH AND ISLAM AND LIVE INSIDE MUSLIM COMMUNITY FOR MAKING PROBLEMS AND EARTHLY BENEFITS.

SO I CAN GIVE 100% GUARANTEE OF SUCCESS IN HEREAFTER IF THE ALL FOUR PART COMPLETE SUCCESSFULLY. IF YOU DON NOT UNDERSTAND ABOUT ALLAH BUT PRACTICED SECOND, THIRD AND FOURTH THINGS TRUTH FULLY YOU HAVE ALSO 100% CHANCE. I CAN NOT GIVE ANY GUARANTY IF A PERSON ONLY PRACTICE THE FIRST ONE.

OUR MAXIMUM AGE IS FIXED AND WRITTEN IN THE PR-WRITTEN DESTINY, BUT WE HAVE LOT OF DIFFERENT DEATH TIMES AT EACH STAGES OF LIFE ALSO. WHICH ARE ALSO WROTE ON PRE-WRITTEN DESTINY. THE CHANCE OF DEATH AT EACH STAGE IS DEPENDS UP ON THAT TIMES LIVE-DESTINY CONDITIONS AND ALLAH ALMIGHTYS APPROVAL. THE MOST OF THE BIOLOGYCAL REASONS FOR DEATH OF OUR BODY ARE

SUDDEN OR GRATUAL CHANGES AND
WEAKNESS IN OUR BODY.

53

CHAPTER-4

54

LIFE AFTER DEATH OR AFTER EARHTLY LIFE

163AS PER OUR AVAILABLE KNOWLEDGE WE ALL KNOWS ONE DAY WE WILL DIE. WE NOT YET SEE ANY PERSON WHO BORN IN THE FIRST GENERATIONS OF HUMANS AND STILL CONTINOUING HIS OR HER LIFE. SO PER OUR SO FAR KNOWLEDGE ONE DAY WE WILL DIE.

ACCORDING TO QURAN "KULLA NAFSUN DHALIKATHUL MOUTH" MEANS EACH BODY TASTE DEATH.

IN THIS CHAPTER I WILL EXPLAIN TWO UNDERSTANDING SYSTEMS ABOUT LIFE AFTER DEATH

FIRST I WILL DISCUSS ABOUT THE PRECENT DAY SALVATION UNDERSTANDING OF MOST OF THE SANADHANADHARMA FOLLOWERS.

ACCORDING TO SALVATION THEORY UNDERSTANDING THE LAST AND SUPREAME STATE OF HUMAN SOUL IS SALVATION STATE. BUT IT IS POSSIBLE ONLY FOR PURIFIED SOULS.

AT FIRST TIME THE POSSIBILITY OF ACHIEVING SUCH STATE IS DEFINED COMMEN FOR EACH PEOPLE OF THE SOCIETY. LATER TIMES SANADHANA DHARMA DEFENITION CHANGED AND IT BECOME DIRECTLY ONLY POSSIBLE FOR BRAHMINS AND THE CAST SYSTEM STARTED.

THEY USED THIS FORMER UNDERSTANDING OF SALVATION FOR THE NEW INTERPRETATION CAST IDENTITY BY USING A NEW THEORY OF VIRAT PURUSHA

(SYMBOLISATION OF GOD BY SANADHANA SCHOLERS) AND START RELATING DIFFERENT CASTS BIRTH IS WITH GODS SYMBOLISED BODY.

SO THE SOUL PURIFICATION SALVATION SYSTEM IS PARTIALY CHANGED BY THE ADDITION OF SOME NEW BELIEFS. ACCORDING TO NEW BELIEF ONLY SOUL IN THE BRAHMINS BODY IS POSSIBLE TO GET DIRECT SALVATION. IF A BRAHMIN LIVE A GOOD PURIFIED LIFE AFTER DEATH HIS OR HER SOUL GETS SALVATION. IF ANY PERSON DIES OTHER THAN A PURIFIED BRAHMIN HE OR SHE WILL GET AGAIN RE BIRTH IN EARTHLY LIFE. ACCORDING TO THAT BAD BRAHMIN AND OTHER CAST BAD PEOPLES WILL RE BIRTH ON LOWER CASTS, GOOD PERSONS FROM OTHER CAST WILL GET UPGRADATION IN THE NEXT BIRTH UP TO GET SALVATION. ACTULLY RE BIRTH IS A REALITY BUT NOT FOR ALL COMMON MANS. THE COMMON REALITY IS ONE EARTHLY LIFE AND SALVATION AT HEAVEN AFTER DEATH.

ACCORDING TO BHAGAVATH GEETHA SREE KRISHNA MOTIVATING ARJUNA BY TELL TO HIM IF YOU DIE IN THE WAR YOU WILL GET PROUD HEAVEN AND IF YOU WIN YOU WILL GET THE THROWN OF POWER AND KINDOM.

THIS MEANS THAT THIS IS THE REAL UNDERSTANDING OF THAT TIMES SOME OF THE SCHOLERS ABOUT HEAR AFTER LIFE.

ACCORDING TO ISLAM WE HAVE ONLY ONE LIFE IN EARTH AS HUMAN, ONLY PROPHETS HAVE THE CHANCE OF GETTING ANOTHER LIFE IF IT IS WRITTEN ON THEIR PRE-WRITTEN DESTINY. AS PER MY UNDERSTANDING PROPHET MUHAMMED HAD EIGHT RE BIRTH IN THE WHOLE PASSED TIME OF HUMEN BEING IN DIFFERENT REGIONS OF EARTH WITH DIFFERENT HUMAN BODYS. AT LAST BIRTH HE BECOME THE MESSENGER OF ALLAH ALMIGHTY.

IF A PERSON DIES MEANS HIS OR HER SOUL TAKEN BY THE ANGEL(MALAK) AND PLACE THE SOUL IN A RESTING PLACE. FROM THAT TIME OUR BODY BECOME DEAD AND STARTED TO DEGRADE. THIS IS WE CALLED AS DEATH.

IF THE PERSON IS PURIFIED PERSON GOD ALMIGHTY TELL HIS ANGEL(MALAK) TO INFORM HIM ABOUT THE HAPPY NEWS OF HEVENLY LIFE, AND PLACE HIS OR HER SOUL IN THE COMMON SOUL RESTING PLACE WITH SOME HEAVENLY FACILITIESE. A FEW PEOPLES GETING THIS TREAT'

IF THE PERSON IS A NON-PURIFIED PERSON GOD ALMIGHTY TELL HIS ANGEL(MALAK) TO INFORM HIM ABOUT THE HARDSHIP OF HELL AND PLACE HIS OR HER SOUL IN THE COMMON SOUL RESTING PLACE WITH SOME FACILITIESE OF HELL. SOME OF THE PEOPLES GETTING THIS TREATMENT.

BUT MOST OF THE PERSON NOT GET ANY INFORMATON ABOUT HELL OR HEAVEN AT THE TIME OF DEATH. ANGEL WILL PLACE THEM IN THE COMMON SOUL RESTING AREA. BUT THEY WILL UNDER GONE THROUGH FEAR BECAUSE OF UNCERTENITY OF THEIR FUTURE. THEIR FINAL DECISION COMES AT THE TIME OF JUDGEMENT DAY AFTER KIYAMATH (LAST HUMAN DAY ON EARTH) DAY ON EARTH.

AT THE TIME OF KIYAMATH DAY NO HUMAN WILL REMAIN AS LIVE.

ALL PEOPLES OF THAT TIMES GENERATIONS WILL DIE. THEN ALLAH ALMIGHTY RE CREATE OUR BODY AND INVITE US TO ENTER IN IT. THAT TIME ALL OF US WILL BECOME BODYLY HUMANS AT A FIXED AGE OF 33.

AS PER MY UNDERSTANDING FROM 2022 AD AROUND 400 SOLAR YEARS REMAINING FOR KIYAMATH DAY.

AFTER KIYAMATH DAY, AT THE TIME OF JUDGEMENT DAY ALLAH WILL DECIDE OUR NEXT DESTINATION AND FUTURE. WITH ALLAH ALMIGHTYS MERCY A BIG PORTION OF HUMANSE WILL ENTER JANNAH (HEAVEN).

A PORTION OF HUMANS WILL PLACE ON HELL.

ALLAH ALMIGHTYS MADE JUDGEMENTS ON US ON THE BASIS OUR GOOD OR BAD ACTIONS.

IF WE REACH HEAVEN WE WILL ALSO REMEMBER OUR EARTHLY LIFE, WE WILL SEARCH OUR FRIEDS AND RELATIEVES THEIR. WE MAY MEET SOME OF THEM THEIR AND SOME OF NOT. ALLAH ALMIGHTY GRANDED PERMISIONS FOR US IN JANNAH FOR REQUISTING THE MISSED PERSONS OF OUR INTEREST. IF THEY ARE NOT IN HEAVEN MEANS THEY ARE IN HELL. ALLAH WILL BRING THEM HEAVEN FOR US BECAUSE ALLAH ALMIGHTY LOVES US. NEW COMERSE HAVE NO PERMISION FOR REQUISTING THEIR INTERESTED ONES FROM HELL. THAT IS ONLY EXCLUSIVE FOR FIRST COMERS.

IN HEAVEN THEIR ALSO OUR AGE IS 33. AND WE ALL GET ONE UNIFORM EXTRABODY WITH ONLY FACE IDENTITY WITH NO GENDER DIFFERENCE. THIS BODY IS REQUIRED US FOR GOING OUT SIDE HEAVEN. WE CAN HIDE ONE OF OUR BODY AT ANY TIME. AFTER A LONG GOOD LIFE AT HEAVEN WE WILL GET PERSION TO CROSS THE ARSH AND PASSESS THROUGH ALLAH ALMIGHTY AND REACH OTHER ARSH-UNIVERSES. LIVING THROUGH ALLAHS SURROUNDING IS RELIGIOUSLY TERMED AS VIEWING ALLAH. THAT IS CONSIDERED AS THE MOST SUPREAME THING OF A HUMAN LIFE. ALL PEOPLES REACH HEAVEN WILL GET ETERNAL LIFE OF PROSPIRITY.

CHAPTER-5

UNDERSTAND BODY-SOUL-MIND

HUMANS ARE SUPERIAR ANIMALS WITH EXTRA ORDINARY SOUL. OUR SPECIALITY IS MORE RELATED TO SOUL THAN OUR BODY. WE KNOW LOT OF HIGHER LIVING ORGANISMS HAVE STRONG BODY, MORE POWER FULL VISION, HEARING CAPACITY, MOVEMENT EBILITY THAN US. SOME OF THEMS INTERNAL ORGANS LIKE BRAIN AND HEART HAVE SOME ADVANTAGES THAN US IN SOME AREAS. IF WE COSIDER ONLY BODY SOME OF THEM ARE MORE ADVANCED THAN US IN SOME AREAS. HUMAN SOUL IS THE MOST ADVANCED AND POWERFULL SOUL AMONGS ALL LIVING ORGANISMS IN THIS UNIVERSE.

SOUL NOT HAVE ANY GENDER DIFFERENCE, SOUL IS A UNISEX ONE FOR EVERY SPECIECES.THE GENDER DIFFERENCE THE DIFFERENCE OF OUR BODY. WE KNOWS HUMANS ARE MAINLY TWO CATEGORY OF GENDERS AND A THIRD ONE TRANSGENDER CATAGORY BODY ARE ALSO PRECENT. A REAL TRANSGENDER MEANS NUTRAL IN BODY SEX.

HUMAN IDENTITY DIAGRAM

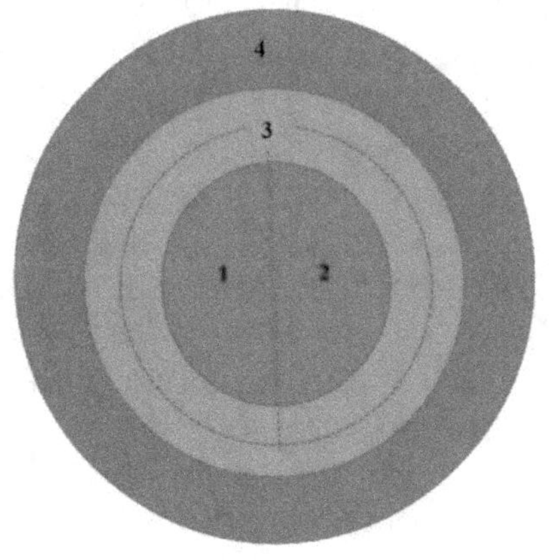

CHAPTER-5: DIAGRAM-1

1) OUR SOUL PORTION WHICH IS NOT IN OUR FULL CONCIOUSNESS AND CONTROL (SYMBOLIC COLOUR RED)

2) OUR SOUL PORTION WHICH LEADING OUR CONCIOUS LIFE (SYMBOLIC COLOUR RED)

3) MIND (SYMBOLIC COLOUR ORANGE)

4) BODY (SYMBOLIC COLOUR GREEN)

IN EARTH AND ENVIRONMENT FIVE CATEGORY OF LIVING AND NON-LIVING THINGS ARE PRECENT.

EARTH.

HUMAN BEING.

ANIMALS AND OTHER LIVING ORGANISMS WITH THE MOTION ABILITY.

VEGITABLES AND PLANTS.
NON-LIVING SUBTANCES.

EARTH: EARTH IS A LIVING CREATION WITH SOUL FROM GOD ALMIGHTY. EARTH OBAYS NATURAL LAWS CREATED BY GOD AND ALSO GOD ALMIGHTYS DIRECT INSTRUCTIONS. THE SOIL, WATER AND STONES ON THE EARTH NOT CONTAINING EARTHS SOUL. THAT IS WHY THEY ARE CONSIDERING THE NON LIVING PART OF EARTH BODY. SUCH THINGS ARE CONTINOUES AS ONLY UNDER THE NATURAL LAWS CREATED BY GOD.

HUMAN BEINGS: IF WE CONSIDER HIGHER LIVING ORGANISMS LIKE ELEPHANT, LION AND EAGLE WE ARE MUCH SUPERIER THAN THEM BECAUSE OF OUR SOUL AND ITS BY-PRODUCT MIND. THEIR SOULS ARE QUALITY-WISE LOWER THAN US, THAT MAKE THE DIFFERENCE.
BEFORE EARTHLY LIFE OF FIRST HUMAN STARTED OUR SOULS WAS MADED AND SEQUIRED IN A SPECIAL SOUL STORAGE AREA.
WHEN WE WILL GET LIFE IN EARTH AS PER PRE-WRITTEN DEATINY OUR SOUL WILL ENTER IN THE BODY GIVEN TO US. FROM THAT TIME OUR SOULS GET ACTIVATION. IN EARTHLY LIFE ONLY A PORTION OF OUR SOUL CAN BE ACESSIBLE AND WORK AS

OUR SELF. THE REMAINING PORTIONS CONTROL WE GET ONLY AFTER OUR DEATH. THE REMAINING PORTION WORKS AS PER THE PRE-INSTALLED HUMAN VALUES AND PROGRAMS WITH LOT OF MEMORY CAPACITY AND WORK AS A INDIRECT COMMUNICATION ZONE BETWEEN SHAITHAN AND OTHER JINNS THROUGH OUR BODY. ALLAH ALMIGHTY COMMUNICATE TO BOTH PORTION OF OUR SOUL NORMALLY THROUGH OUR BRAIN.

OUR MIND IS THE INTERACTION ZONE BETWEEN OUR BODY AND SOUL. MIND IS A COMBINATION OF BOTH BODY AND SOUL. IF WE CONSIDER OUR TOTAL IDENTITY AS 100 % MIND POSESS 30% TO 40% CONTROLL DIRECTLY. THE REMAINING IS CONTROLLED BOTH DIRCTLY AND INDIRECTLY BY REMAINING PORTION OF BODY AND SOUL. IN THE FIRST CHAPTER I AM GIVEN A BRIEF KNOWLEDGE ABOUT THIS, THAT WILL ALSO HELPS TO UNDERSTANT THIS POINTS.

OUR SOUL IS MAINLY SPREDED AT THE UPPER BODY. FROM FRONT SIDE STARTING POINT OF NECK WITH BOTH SOULDER TO CHEST CENTRE AND AT THE BACK SIDE BOTH SHOULDER TO LOWER POINT OF OUR BACKBORN. AT BOTH SIDE UP TO MIDLE PORTION SPRED AREA IS WIDED AS THE SHOULDER PORTION. AT THE LOWER MIDDLE PORTION SPRED AREA IS OUTWARD

CURVLY CENTERED TO BOTH CENTER POINTS.

OUR SOUL NOT HAVE ANY PRECENT OR SPRED IN OUR HEAD AS WELL AS IN THE LOWER BODY, BELOW THE WAIST AREA. USUALLY GOD ALMIGHTYS HOLLY SOUL USES OUR HEAD AREA TO COMMUNICATE WITH OUR SOUL. CREATIONS LIKE JINS (A TYPE OF CREATION FROM GOD ALMIGTHY, THEIR BODY MADE UP OF FIRE, LIKE HUMANS BOTH GOOD AND BAD JINS ARE PRECENT IN THIS WORLD) SOME TIME USESES OUR WHOLE BODY FOR THEIR INTERACTION WITH OUR BODY AND SOUL.

SOUL IS A PHYSICAL ENTITY MADE UP OF A HIGHER NEXT STATE OF PLASMA. SOUL INTERACT WITH OUR BODY MOSTLY THROUG OUR NERVE SYSTEMS.

IT IS LESS WEIGHTED AND POWERFUL THAN PLASMA STATE. SOUL CAN MOVE FASTER THAN LIGHT ALSO. WHEN SOUL RESIDES IN THE BODY SOUL WILL NOT TRAVEL OUT SIDE OF BODY, IF THAT HAPPENDS MEANS DEATH HAPPENDS TO OUR BODY. AS PER QURAN AT THE TIME OF OUR SLEEP OUR IDENTITY SOUL PORTIONS CONTROLS ALSO CONTROLED BY ALLAH ALMIGHTY.

IN EARLY CHAPTERS I EXPLAINED ABOUT THE SOUL CAPACITY, IT MEANS THE MEMORY CAPACITY, PROGRAAM CAPACITY AND SKILL CAPACITY OF THE SOUL, EXEPT PROGRAAM CAPACITY AND TOTAL

CAPACITY WE CAN IMPROOVE OUR SOUL KNOWLEDGE AND SKILLS. PROGRAAM (SOULS WORKING NATURE CAPACITY) AND TOTAL CAPACITYS UPGRADATION AND DOWNGRADATION ARE BELONGS TO GOD ALMIGHTYS DIRECT CONTROL.

I WILL GIVE SOME IDEA ABOUTS MINDS PROPORTION ALSO, I BEFORE EXPLAINED MIND POSESS 40% CONTROL OF OUR LIFE, ACTUALLY MIND IS THE CONCIOUNESS RESIDING SPACE OF US.

WE KNOW ABOUT OUR BODY, BUT WE DO NOT NORMALLY KNOWS ITS WORKING PRINCIPLES, AND ALSO WE ARE NOT CONTROLING SUCH THINGS CONCIOUSLY. MOST OF THAT ARE WORKING UNDER OUR SOULS AUTOMATED CONTROL SYSTEM THROGH NERVE SYSTEMS. THAT ARE BELONGS TO THE BEYOND OUR CONTROL PORTION OF SOUL.

OUR BODY AND SOUL ARE MUTUALLY CONNECTED TO OUR BODY, OUR SOUL AND OUTSIDE ENVIRONMENT IN THE CASE OF EXPOSURE AND EXPERIENCE. IF WE SEE SOMETHING, IF WE HEAR SOMETHING THAT WILL MAKE REACTIONS AT BODY, SOUL AND MIND IN DEFERENT PROPOTION. THESE REACTIONS DIFFERENCE TO PERSON BY PERSON. I CAN GIVE SITUATION EXAMPLES IF WE MET OUR LOVER, AND STAY AT HIS OR HER PRESENCE OUR HORMON PRODUCTION MAY VARY COMPARED TO OTHER

SITUATIONS. ANOTHER SITUATION IF SEE SUDDENLY SOMETHING EXTREAMLY FEARFULL LIKE A MUDER, ETC YOU MAY BECOME PARALYSE FOR SOME MOMENTS. IF WE ATTENDING A HIGH PRIORITY BUSINESS OR POLITICAL MEATING WITH A SECOND PARTY COMMUNICATIONS HAPPENDS THEIR WILL MAKE CHANGES IN BODY-SOUL AND MIND. THESE ALL BECAUSE OF THAT EYE SIGHTS AND HEARINGS AFFECTING OUR SOUL DIRECTLY MORE THAN OUR BODY THROUGH OUR ORGANS THAT WILL SOMETIMES GIVE A POSITIVE RISE, SOMETIMES GIVE SHOCKS AND SOME TIMES IMPROVEMENTS. SO REGULAR PRACTICES ON SUCH SITUATIONS WILL IMPROVE OUR PERFORMANCES OF SUCH KIND OF SITUATIONS IN FUTURE. MEANS THAT WILL DEVELOPE OUR MIND.

AT USUAL TIME OUR ACTIONS AND THOUGHTS ARE DIRECTLY MOSTLY CONTROLLED BY OUR BODY AND INDIRECTLY BY OUR SOUL. AT VIGILANT AND ENLIGHTED TIME ACTION AND THOUGHTS ARE MORE DIRECTLY CONTROLLED BY OUR MIND AND SOUL. THE PERSENTAGE OF USUAL AND VIGILANT TIME WILL VARY WITH PERSON BY PERSON AND IT DIRECTLY RELATED TO THEIR EXPOSURE AREAS AND THEIR PERSONALITY.

IMAGIN A CAR AND DRIVER SET UP, CAR RUNNING THROUGH A HIGHWAY. WE ARE

DRIVING THE CAR MEANS OUR SOUL, CAR IS OUR BODY.

OUR EFFORT AND EFFORT OF THE CONTROLING AND RUNNING SYSTEM OF CAR MAKES THE MIND.

WE, HOLLY SOUL AND JINN'S RELATION A SYMBOLIC DIAGRAM

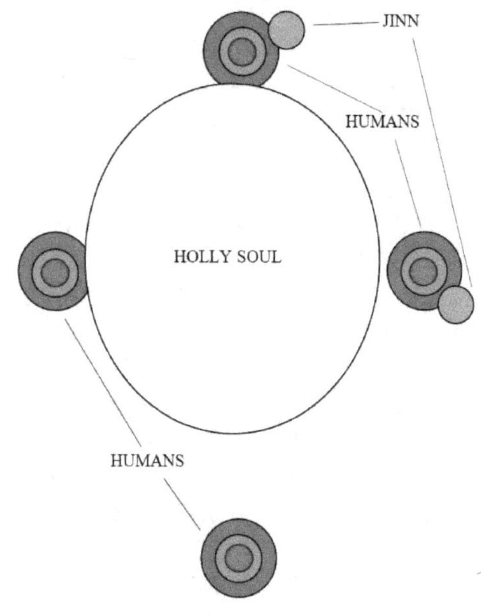

CHAPTER-5 DIAGRAM-2

ANIMALS AND OTHER LIVING ORGANISM WITH MOTION ABILITY: ALL ANIMALS AND MICRO ORGANISMS HAVE SOUL IN THEIR BODY WITH DIFFERENT QUALITY CATAGORYS. ONE SPECIESE ANIMAL SOUL IS DIFFERENT FROM OTHER SPECIESES. ONE

CATEGORY OF ANIMAL MEANS THEIR BODY AND SOUL ARE DIFFERENT FROM OTHER ANIMAL GROUPS.

I CAN GIVE A CATEGORY EXAMPLE, CAT GROUP ANIMALS LIKE TIGER, LION, CAT, JAGUAR ETC HAVE SAME QUALITY SOULS, THEIR BEHAVIOR DIFFERENCE IS DUE TO THEIR SELF IMAGE AND BODY CHARACTERISTICS. THEIR BODY PROPORTION DIFFERENCES HAPPENED DUE TO THE DIFFERENT PROPORTION OF EVOLUTION HAPPENED THROUGH THEIR COMMON ANCESTRAL CHAIN.

HIGHER ANIMALS HAVE MIND, LOVER MICRO ORGANISMS DO NOT HAVE MIND.

VEGETABLES AND PLANTS: PLANTS HAVE ONLY SOUL AND BODY, THEY HAVE NO MIND. VEGETABLES AND PLANTS HAVE LOW QUALITY SOUL COMPARE WITH ANIMAL WORLD. DIFFERENT BODYS CATOGARY VEGETABLES AND PLANTS POSESS DIFFERENT CATEGORY SOULS. PLANTS HAVE MORE NATURAL LIFE PRESERVATION SUSTAINIBITY THAN ANIMALS EVEN AFTER REMOVE FROM THE SOURCE, BECAUSE PLANTS LIFE IS MORE RELATED TO PLANTS BODY THAN SOUL.

NON-LIVING SUBSTANCES: NON LIVING SUBSTANCES DO NOT HAVE MIND AND SOUL THEY HAVE ONLY BODY, EXAMPLES FOR

NON LIVING SUBSTANCES ARE COPPER, IRON, STONE, SOIL, WATER, ETC. THEY ARE CONTINOUING IN THIS UNIVERSE AS PER THE NATURAL LAWS IMPLIMENTED BY THE GOD ALMIGHTY. AS LIKE SOULED LIVING ORGANISMS THEY DO NOT HAVE ANY THINKING OR DECISION MAKING POWER.

GOD ALMIGHTY CREATED AND CREATING THIS UNIVERSE INSIDE THE ARSH THROUGH DIFFERENT STAGES AND GOD IMPLEMENT MOTION AND EVOLUTION TO GOD ALMIGHTY'S CREATIONS EVERY WHERE.

CHAPTER-6

HUMAN EVOLUSION ISLAMIC UNDERSTANDINGS

EVOLUTION IS THE WORD GET WIDE POPULARITY IN MODERN TIME OF SCIENCE AFTER CHARLS DARWIN. HE PROPOSED A THEORY WHICH DESCRIBES THE CHANCE OF EVOLUSION IN LIVING WORLD.

HE OBSERVED THAT CHANGES HAPPENING IN THE LIVING WORLD THROUGH NATURAL SELECTION AND SOME OF THEM TRANSFERING TO NEXT GENERATION AND THE PROCESS IS CONTINOUING IN THE PRECENT TIME ALSO. LATER DARWINIST SCHOOL OF THEORYST TRACE BACK THE BEGINNING OF LIVING WORLD TO A SINGLE CELL MICRO ORGANISM. AS PER THEIR THEORY THEY CLAIM THAT THROUGH GENERATIONS OF DIFFERENT STAGES OF EVOLUSION WITH DIFFERENT PROPORTION LEADS TO THE FORMATION OF DIFFERENT LIVING ORGANISMS INCLUDING HIGHER ANIMALS OF THE WORLD.

THEY CATOGARISED EVOLUTION HAPPENDED AS TWO MAIN CATOGORY MICRO EVOLUTION AND MACRO EVOLUSION. MACRO EVOLUSION MEANS A CATEGORY OR SPECIESE OF LIVING ORGANISM EVOLUTED TO ANOTHER SPECIOUS THROUGH CONTINOUS NATURAL SELECTION OF THEIR ANCESTRAL GENERATIONS. IN NOW A DAYS SOME DARWIN SCHOOL OF EVOLUSION THEORYST BELIEVES IN SUDDEN CHANGES ALSO. MICRO EVOLUSION MEANS SMALL

CHANGES HAPPENING IN A CATEGORY OR SPECIOUS DUE TO EVOLUSION THROUGH NATURAL SELECTION. ACCORDING TO DARWINIST THEORY OF INTERPRETATION OF LIVING WORLD, EXAMPLE FOR MICRO EVOLUSION IS DIFFERENT ETHNICITYS OF MAN KIND. ACCORDING TO THEIR MACRO EVOLUSION INTERPRETATION I WILL GIVE A MY SIDE INTERPRETATION EXAMPLE LIKE LIONS ARE EVOLVED FROM HUMANS. WE KNOW BOTH ARE TWO CATEGORY OR SPECIECE, AND HUMANS ARE EVOLVED FROM ELEPHANT. THEY CAN NOT DENAY MY INTERPRETATION BECAUSE THEY EVEN DO NOT HAVE SCIENTIFIC PROF OR EVIDENCE WHAT THEY EXAMPLED.

ACTUALLY MY UNDERSTANDING ABOUT EVOLUSION IS MICRO EVOLUTION IS ONLY HAPPENDS AND HAPPENING IN THE LIVING WORLD.

THE CONCEPT OF MACRO EVOLUSION IS A UNAUTHENTIC AND FALLS ONE.

I WILL DISCUSS HOW MICRO EVOLUTION HAPPENS AND THE CHANCE OF NATURAL SELECTION WITH A BRIEF STUDY OF HUMAN HISTORY. FIRST I WILL DISCUSS THE ISLAMIC STAND. ACCORDING TO ISLAM ALLAH ALMIGHTY CREATED THE EARTHLY LIVING ORGANISMS AT DIFFERENT STAGES. ALLAH ALMIGHTY CREATED THIS ARSH- UNIVERSE SYSTEM 72 BILLION EARTH YEARS BEFORE. EARTH AND SOLAR SYSTEM CREATED 3

BILLION EARTH YEARS BEFORE (SOME ONE WILL ARISE A DOUT, BEFORE EARTH CREATION HOW CALCULATING THE EARTH YEAR, MY ANSWER IS I AM JUST USING IT AS A COMMUNICATION UNIT BECAUSE WE ALL KNOW IT). THE FIRST LIVING THING CREATED TO PLACE ON EARTH WAS HAPPENED 2 BILLION EARTH YEARS BEFORE. FIRST HUMAN BODY ANIMAL CREATED AROUND 5 LACK YEARS BEFORE.

FIRST REAL HUMAN THE ADAM AND HIS FAMILY CREATED AROUND 1.5 LACK YEARS BEFORE. SO MEANY DIFFERENT CATEGORY OR SPECIOUS OF PLANTS, ANIMALS AND OTHER LIVING ORGANISMS ARE CREATED ON EARTH BEFORE ADAM AND AFTER ADAM ALSO. ALLAH ALMIGHTY CREATING THE LIVING WORLD AS DIFFERENT CATEGORY OR SPECIOUSE AT DIFFERENT STAGES ON EARTH AND FREE THE CATEGORY OR SPECIOUSE LIFE'S UNDER THE NATURAL LAW OF EVOLUTION AND DESTINY(QADHR).

MACRO EVOLUSION IS A NON-REAL THING UNDER ISLAMIC UNDERSTANDING, BUT MICRO EVOLUSION IS A REALITY. IN A CHAPTER OF QURAN ALLAH ALMIGHTY INFORM US THAT AT A PREVIOUS TIME ALLAH GIVE SOME UPLIFTMENT IN JEWISH COMMUNITY BY GIVING THEM SPECIAL FOOD AND FECILITIESE FOR THEIR SOME GENERATIONS. THESE WORDS MEANS THAT A MICRO EVOLUSION OF POSITIVE CHANGE

HAPPENED IN THAT SOCIETY THROGH INDIRECT ACTION FROM GOD ALMIGHTY.

ACCORDING TO MY UNDERSTANDING THE FACTORS AFFECTING NEGATIVE OR POSITIVE MICRO EVOLUSIONS IN HUMAN LIFE ARE

1) FOOD
2) WHETHER
3) NATURE OF WORK
4) MENTAL AND SOUL STATE
5) LAND SCAPE OF THE REGION

SO THESE ARE THE MAIN FACTORS OF NATURAL SELECTION.

NOW I WILL GIVE A BRIEF HISTORY OF HUMAN BEING WITH THE HELP OF OBSERVATION, ISLAMIC KNOWLEDGE AND GOD ALMIGHTYS HOLLY SOULS TEACHINGS.

I AM UNDERSTOOD THAT PROPHET ADAM IS THE FIRST REAL HUMAN AND FIRST PROPHET OF GOD ALMIGHTY. ALLAH ALMIGHTY CREATED ADAM AND HIS WIFE HAWWA FOR THE EARTH, ALLAH THEN PLACED THEM AT HEAVEN BECAUSE ALLAH HAVE SOME PLAN, ADAM AND HAWWA FAILED IN SOME MEANS IN THE MATTER OF OBAYING GOD ALMIGTHY. SO ALLAH SHOWED THEM THE NEXT OPTION, THAT IS RETUR BACK TO EARTHLY LIFE.

AT FIRST ALLAH PLACE BOTH OF THEM AT DIFFERENT REGIONS OF EARTH. ADAM IS PLACED AT A OLD NON-EXISTING CONTINET

NEAR PRECENT DAY INDONESIA. AND HAWWA IS PLACED NEAR PRECENT DAY YEMEN. BOTH OF THEM SPEND THEIR LIFE ALONE FOR YEARS. AFTER SOME YEARS ADAM GET GOD ALMIGHTYS HELP AND COME TO NEAR YEMEN AND MEET HIS COUPLE HAWWA. THIS IS CONSIDERED AS THE RE-UNION AND BEGINIG OF FIRST HUMAN FAMILY ON EARTH. PROPHET ADAM BECOME FATHER AND HAWWA BECOME MOTHER.

TIMES PASSESS NEW GENERATIONS OF HUMANS BORN, BROUGHT UP AND DIED AT EARTH. THAT TIME HUMAN AVERAGE AGE WAS AROUND 100YEARS. THOUSAND OF YEARS PASSED AND SO MEANY GENERATIONS LIVED OF THEIR FOR FATHERS LAND NEAR YEMEN. DUE TO DIFFERENT REASONS SMALL GROUPS OF THE FIRST SOCIETY STARTED TO SEPARATE FROM THEIR FOREFATHERS SOCITY AND SETTLED IN ANOTHER AREAS LONG AWAY FROM THE STARTING POINT. MOST OF THE GROUPS STAY LONG AWAY FROM OTHER GROUPS BECAUSE OF SAFETY REASONS AND THEY FIND NEW BETTER DESTINATIONS FOR THEIR FREEDOM OF LIFE. THESE DIFFERENT SMAL GROUPS BECOME BIG SOCITYS THROUGH THOUSANDS OF YEARS AND STILL SPIT-UP AND NEW GROUP FORMATION AND NEW SETTLEMENT CONTINOUES. SOME

SETTLED MORE THAN 5000KM FROM THEIR STARTING SOCIETYS.

TEN THOUSAND, TWENTY THOWSAND AND THIRTY THOUSAND YEARS PASSESS THESE NEW SOCIETYS BECOME NEW ETHNICITYS THROUH EVOLUSION BY NATURAL SELECTION. THE BEFORE EXPLAINED POINTS OF MICRO EVOLUSION FACTORS OF THEIR LIFE MAKES THE LEADING RESON FOR EVOLUSION. DIFFERENT AREAS ENVIRONMENT, FOOD, WHETHER AND NATURE OF WORK CHANGED THE HUMAN BODY GRATUALLY THROUGH LONG GENERATION TIME

FROM THE BEGINNING TIME WITH IN THIRTY THOWSAND YEARS HUMAN SOCIETYS SPRED ALL MOST AREAS OF EARTH. BUT A DIFFERENCE WITH NOW A DAYS ARE EACH GROUP KEEP SAFE DISTANCE OF THOUSANDS OF KILOMETERS FROM OTHER GROUPS. THE COMMUNICATION BETWEEN DIFFERENT GROUPS ARE RARE AT THAT TIME. THEY ARE MOSTLY REVOLED INSIDE THEIR GROUPS ONLY. EVOLUSION AND HUMAN SOCIAL ACHIEVEMENTS ALSO PROGRESSED. ONE SOCIETYS ACHIEVEMENT AND DEVELOPMENT DID NOT FASTLY SPRED TO OTHER SOCIETYS BECAUSE OF THIR NON-RELATIONS WITH THE OTHER SOCITYS. ALL SOCITYS GET MESSENGERS OF ALLAH ALL MIGHTY IN DIFFERENT TIMES, AFTER FIRST THIRTY THOUSAND YEARS EACH

SOCITY BECOME SEPARATE ETHNIC PEOPLE AND PEOPLES OF DISTINCT CULTURE.

THAT TIME ALLAH GIVE MORE COMMUNICATION POWER TO HUMAN SOUL TO ANIMAL SOUL. PEOPLES OF DIFFERENT SOCITIES STARTED TO MAKE MORE RELATIONS WITH THE ANIMALS SAME TIME ANIMALS ALSO ATTRACTED TO HUMANS. CENTURYS PASSESS MICRO EVOLUSION CONTINOUS IN DIFFERENT HUMAN SOCIETYS AT DIFFERENT PROPORTIONS.

GENERATIONS PASSESS, ANGELS AND ALLAH ALMIGHTYS HOLLY SOUL OBSERVED THAT MOST OF THE HUMAN SOCITYS STARTED TO LIVE IN WRONG WAYS AND SOCIAL LIFE BECOME WORST. THAT TIME MORE THAN 100 PURE HUMAN ETHNIC SOCITYS ARE PRECENT AT EARTH.

ALLAH ALMIGTHYS HOLLY SOUL PLAN A STRONG INVOLMENT AS PER THE OPTIONS OF THE PRE-WRITTEN DESTINY. ALLAH STRICTLY UTILISE SOME OPTIONS AND MADE SOME CHANGES IN THE HUMAN CIVILISATIONS, OTHER WISE HUMANS CAN NOT EXIST LIKE OLD HUMAN BODY ANIMAL, BECAUSE OF INTERNAL PROBLEMS AND CLASHES.

ALLAH ALMIGHTYS HOLLY SOUL PREPARED SOME TEACHERS AND GUIDES FROM EACH HUMAN SOCIETY AND AWARE THEM ABOUT THE BAD AND GOOD OF HUMAN LIFE. THIS IS HAPPENDS AROUND ONE LACK YEARS

AFTER PROPHET ADAM. BUT MOST MISSIONS ARE FAILED PEOPLES CONTINOUE IN A WAY WHAT THEY INTERESTED. ACTUALLY THAT TIMES PEOPLS MOST INTEREST ARE BELONGS TO BAD BECAUSE OF THAT TIMES SOCIAL SITUATIONS.

ALLAH ALMIGHTYS HOLLY SOUL DICIDED TO REMOVE MOST OF THE HUMAN SOCITYS THROGH THE OPTIONS AVAILABLE IN THE PRE-WRITTEN DESTINY BECAUSE MOST OF THEM BECOME CRIMINALS.

AROUND 40000 YEARS BEFORE OUR TIMES ALLAH ALMIGHTYS HOLLY SOUL SELECT A SOCIETY FOR FINAL CHANCE FOR EXISTENCE, BECAUSE THEY HAVE LITTLE BIT GOOD SOCIAL CONDITION IN THEIR SOCIETY. AND PLANNED REMAINING SOCIETY TO REMOVE.

PROPHET NOHA WAS INTRODUCED TO THAT SOCIETY AS LIKE EVERY MANS PRE-DESTINY. IN THAT TIME OF PROPHET NOHA HE AND SOME OF HIS GENERATIONS LIVED A LIFE SPAN MORE THAN NORMAL GENERATIONS. IT HAPPENED FOR PROPHET NOHAHS GENERATION TO NEXT 10 OR 11 GENERATION OF THE SOCIETY. PROPHET NOHAS GENERATIONS LIVE AROUND 900 YEARS THE REMAINING 10 GENERATIONS LIVE UP TO PROPHET NOHAS LIFE TIME BUT LESS THAN HIS GENERATION.

THAT MEANS PROPHET NOHAH GET MORE THAN 15 GENERATIONS FOR HIS REACH.

PROPHET NOHAS RELIGIOUS MISSION MOST OF HIS SCOCITY MEMBERS REJECTED INCLUDING HIS WIFE. HE GOT VERY FEW RELIGIOUS PRACTINERS.

THE MISSION TIMING WAS ALL MOST FINISHED ALLAH ALMIGHTYS HOLLY SOUL DIRECT HIM FOR BUILD A SMALL SHIP SUFFICIENT FOR SEA TRAVEL.

AS PER GOD ALMIGHTYS INSTRUCTION PROPHET NOHAH AND HIS COLLEAGES BUILD A SHIP, AND THE INSTRUCTED SHIP LOCATION WAS AT THE TOP OF A HILL. BECAUSE THIS IS A DIVIDING TIME IF SOME ONE SEE PROPHET NOHAS ACTION THEY WILL CALL HAS A MENTALLY ILLED ONE, EVEN PROPHET NOHA DO NOT SURE THAT WHY GOD TELL HIM TO BUILD A SHIP AT THE TOP OF THE HILL. AFTER SHIP BUILDING ALLAH ALMIGHTYS HOLLY SOUL INFORM HIM TO INVITE PEOPLES FOR A ESCAPE JOURNEY. MOST OF THE MEMBERS OF HIS SOCIETY REJECT HIM AND CALLED HIM AS A FOOL.

THEN ALLAH ALMIGHTYS HOLLY SOUL CONFIRMED ALL SOCITYS CONDITION, INCLUDING PROPHET NOHAS.

PROPHET NOHAH AND SOME OF HIS COMPANIANS WITH THEIR ANIMALS START THE PREPARATION OF THE JOURNEY AND COME TO THE SHIP. AFTER SOMETIME ALLAH ALMIGHTY HOLLY SOUL MAKE A SPECIAL RAIN WHICH LAST UP TO A WEAK.

PROPHET NOHAH AND HIS COMPANIANS SAFELY SPEND AT SHIP AND THE WATER LEVEL REACHES THE TOP OF THE HILL SHIP STARTED TO MOOVE. A MASSIVE FLOOD HAPPENED EVERY WHERE, PROPHET NOHAS SHIP TRAVELLED SUCCESSFULLY OVER THE WATER BODY AND AFTER A WEAK SHIP RESTED IN A PLACE, THE RAIN STOPPED AND FLOOD GRATUALLY DISAPEARED. PROPHET NOHA AND HIS COMPANIONS CONTINUE THEIR LIFE, ALL THE REMAINING HUMAN BEINGS AND A PORTION OF ANIMALS DIED IN THE MASSIVE FLOOD.

THIS WAS A TURNING POINT IN HUMAN HISTORY. PROPHET NOHAS SHIP REST NEAR TO PRECENT DAY ANDAMAN AND NIKOBAR ISLAND OF INDIA. THAT TIME ANDAMAN AND NIKOBAR, SOUTH INDIAN PORTION AND BALI OF INDONATIA IS A UNITED CONTINET SITUATED IN BETEEN ANDAMAN AND BALI.

FROM THEIR NEW STAGE OF HUMAN LIFE STARTED. THAT TIME ONLY ONE HUMAN ETHNITY AND CULTURE EXIST THAT IS PROPHET NOHAS AND HIS COMPANIANS SOCIETY. FROM THIS SOCIETY AGAIN SEPERATION AND LONG AWAY SETTLEMENT STARTED AFTER SO MEANY GENERATIONS.

PRECENT DAY WE ARE ALL AROUND THE WORLD. NOW WE ARE DIVIDED AS EIGHT MAJOR PURE ETHINIC GROUPS AND HUNDREDS OF SUB ETHNICITYS AND DECENSE OF CROSS-ETHNICITIES.

THE PURE ETHNIC GROUPS ARE
1)DRAVIDIAN
2)MANGOLIAN
3)ARYAN
4)ASYRYAN
5)EUROPEAN
6)NEGRO
7)MALAYAN, AND
8)NATIVE AMERICAN

ALL THESE PURE GROUPS CONTAINS SO MANY SUB-ETHNIC GROUPS

THE REMAINING ETHNICITYS ARE THE CROSS-BREEDED MIXED ETHINICITYS.
THE ETHNIC PEOPLES MORE RELATED TO PROPHET NOHAS SOCIETY ARE DRAVIDENCE. THEY ARE COMPARITIVLY LESS CHANGED FROM PROPHET NOHAS GENERATIONS.
AFTER THIRTY THOUSAND YEARS OF PROPHET ADAMS AND UPTO PROPHET NOHAS GENERATION HUMANS HAVE MORE COMMUNICATION EBILITYS WITH ANIMALS NOT THROUH TOUG THRUGH SOUL INTIMACY. AFTER PROPHET NOHAS GENERATION ALLAH ALMIGHTYS HOLLY SOUL REDUCE OUR THAT CAPABILITY GRATUALLY.
AS PER MY UNDERSTANDING AROUND FOUR HUNDRED YEARS REMAINING FOR

KIYAMATH DAY THE LAST DAY OF HUMANS IN EARTH.

SO FAR I EXPLAINED ABOUT THE EVOLUTION AND HUMAN EVOLUTION OF BODY. OUR BODY IS COMING THROGH THE CHAIN OF OUR ANCESTRIAL GENERATIONS, ACHIEVING ALL GOOD BODY EVOLUTION CHANGES IS NORMALLY NOT POSSIBLE IN OUR SINGLE LIFE TIME. ITS TOTALITY IS THE RESULT OF HUNDREDS OF GENERATIONS.

NOW I WILL DISCUSS ABOUT THE SPIRITUAL AND MENTAL EVOLUTION AND PROGRESS.

AVERAGE HUMAN BEING IS AN ANIMAL OF GOOD SELF IMAGE AND UNDERSTANDING. IF WE COMPARE OUR SELF WITH BIGGEST ANIMAL OF LAND ELEPHANT WE HAVE MORE SELF IMAGE AND UNDERSTANDING ABOUT OUR SELF THAN ELEPHANTS ABOUT THEM. WE ARE COMPARITIVELY MORE KNOWS ABOUT OUR STRENTH AND WEAKNESSESS. A PERSON WHO KNOWS ABOUT THEM IN THIS WAY HAVE MORE CHANCE TO SUCCED THAN OTHERS.

I WILL GIVE SOME EXAMPLES OF OTHER VERY IMPORTANT THING SELF CONTROL.

ASSUME WE HAVE A CAR, WE WANT TO GO FOR A URGENT MEETING.

WHEN WE START THE CAR WE UNDESTOOD THAT ITS BRAKE IS NOT WORKING PROPERLY. CAN WE USE THAT CAR FOR OUR PURPOSE? NO.

WHY? IT HAS NO BRAKES. LIKE VEHICLES BRACKING SYSTEM OUR SELF-. CONTROL AND EMOTIONAL CONTROL GIVES US THE ABILITY TO DEALING WITH DIFFERENT ENVIRONMENTS. IT GIVES CAPABILITY TO US TO STAND IN OUR POSITION AT DIFFICULT SITUATIONS. IT GIVES STABILITY IN MOVEMENTS AND PROGRESS.

I WILL GIVE ANOTHER EXAMPLE, SUPPOSE WE ARE RIDING A BIKE THROUGH A TWO WAY HIGHWAY. WHAT ARE THE THINGS WE CONCIOUSLY AND SUB-CONCIOUSLY CHECK. FIRST OF ALL OUR DIRECTION OF TRAVEL, THEN ANY OBSTACLES IS THEIR OR NOT, SURROUNDING VEHICLES RELATIVE SPEED, ETC. AT THE TIME OF RIDE SUPPOSE WE MAKE AN ACCIDENT BY HIT A POST SIDE TO THE HIGH WAY OR TO A VEHICLE, CAN WE CALL US A GOOD CONTROLLED RIDER OR MAN OF GOOD SELF CONTROL. BECAUSE WE ALL KNOWS LIFE IS NOT A SINGLE HIGH WAY SINGLE VEHICLE JOURNEY. IT IS SURE WE SHOULD FACE SOME OBSTRUCLES AND DIFFICULTIESE. ACTUALLY TO THESE REASONABLE DIFFICULTIESE AND OBSTRUCLES MAKE US STRONG. WITH OUT SUCH EXPOSURE WE WILL NEVER BECOME STRONG AND EFFICIENT PERSON.

I KNOW SOMEBODY WILL FACE DIFFICULTIES IN SOME NEW EXPOSED SITUATIONS. IF YOU DID NOT MAKE CONTROL OVER SUCH SITUATIONS MEANS

YOU CAN NOT PROGRESS FURTHER AT THAT DIRECTION. SO THROUGH THIS EXPERIENCES WE SHOULD DEVELOPE OUR SKILL AND KNOWLEDGE AND BECOME A EXPERT IN THAT MATTER.

WE SHOULD CONSIDER OUR PERSONAL AND FAMILY LIFE AS VERY IMPORTANT MATTER AND A WAY OF GETTING PEACE AND WISDOM.

MY ADVICE IS, IF YOU LIKE THE PRESENCE OF A LADY OR MEN YOU SHOULD SELECT ONE AND MAKE HER OR HIM AS YOUR LIFE PARTNER.

I AM NOT A SUPPORTER OF SAME GENDER MARRIAGE, OPPOSITE GENDER MARRIAGE IS THE RIGHT AND REAL MARRIAGE. AS PER ISLAMIC UNDERSTANDING IF YOU MAKE A MARRIGE WITH APROPRIATE PARTNER AND LIVE THE LIFE WITH VIRTUE, GOOD VALUES, PEACE AND WISDOM MEANS YOU COMPLETE MORE THAN HALF OF THE RELIGION.

FOR MARRIAGE MY SUJETION IS THE COUPLES SHOULD BE A FOLLOWER OF SAME IDEOLOGY OR SAME CULTURE OR BOTH. THE REMAINING ARE PERSONAL AND FAMILY CHOICES OF THE INDIVITUALS.

NOW I AM DISCUSSING ABOUT THE RELIGIOUS INNER SOUL MEANS RELIGIOUS MENTAL AND SPIRITUAL PROGRESS

RELIGIOUS PRACTICES HAVE TWO TYPE OF BENEFITS. ONE IS AS LIKE EVERY GOOD ACTIONS IT BENEFITS US, ACTUALLY THIS PART IS MORE RELATED TO OUR MIND AND PHYSICAL WELL BEING. THE SECOND PART IS THE MOST PRECIOUS ONE THAT IS ALLAH ALMIGHTYS HOLLY SOULS NEARNESS WITH OUR SOUL.

FOR ACHIEVING ALL THESE BENEFITS AND SUPREAM STATE WE SHOULD PRACTICE DHAIWAVABODHAM (GOD CONCIOUSNESS) AND IBADATH.

DHAIWAVABODHAM (GOD CONSIOUSNESS) STATE WE SHOULD MAINTAIN FOR TRANSFORM OUR ALL ACTIONS AS GOOD ACTIONS AND THEN TRANSFORM ALL GOOD ACTIONS TO IBADHATH (ACTIONS LIKES BY ALLAH ALMIGHTY AND WHICH SHOULD PERFORMED ON ALLAH ALMIGHTY LIKED WAY)

THE BRIEF DEFINITION OF DHAIWAVABODHAM (GOD CONSCIOUSNESS) IS "WE DID NOT SEEING ALLAH ALMIGHTY BUT ALLAH ALMIGHTY SEEING US"

IF WE GET ALLAH ALMIGHTYS NEARNESS, ALLAH ALMIGHTYS HOLLYS SOUL WILL MAKE A CONCIOUS COMMUNICATION PATH WITH OUR SOUL.

AND HOLLY SOUL WILL GUID US IN OUR LIFE.

THE PATH OF GETTING GOD ALMIGHTYS NEARNESS IS DOING IBADATH (PRAYERS AND GOOD ACTIONS WITH THE NIYATH) UNDER DHAIWAVABODHAM (GOD CONCIOUSNESS).

IBADATHS ARE CLASSIFIED AS TWO CATEGORYS ONE IS RILIGIOUS PRAYERS AND RITUALS THESE ARE FORMAL IBADATHS. THESE CONSIST OF

SALAH (PRAYER AT MASJIDH OR HOME) ONE MONTH DAY TIME FASTING AT THE MONTH OF RAMADHAN

HAJJ-PILGRIMAGE AT HOLLY CITY OF MECCA AT THE MONTH OF DHUL HAJ

SAKATH-FINANCIAL ASSET PURIFICATION TAX, PEOPLE WHO HAVE A SPECIFIC QUANTITY OF ASSET SHOULD DISTRIBUTE IT WITH THE ALIGIBLE ZAKATH CLASSIFICATION CATOGORY PEOPLES. IT IS AROUND 2.5 PERCENTAGE OF THE ASSET MINIMUM, IF IT IS POSSIBLE THEY CAN GIVE MORE AS SADAKA OF GIFT.

AND MAINTAIN PEACE AND HARMONEY IN FAMILY AND SOCIETY.

THESE ARE THE FIVE FORMAL IBADATHS MUSLIMS SHOULD PRACTICE. AS PER MY UNDERSTANDING IT CONSIST OF 50% PORTION OF IBADATH BY NATURE.

THESE ALL PRAYERS AND ACTIONS BECOME IBADATH THROUGH PROPER NIYATHS AT

THE BEGINNING. NIYATH IS A BEGINNING PLEDGE AT EACH IBADATH BY SUBMITING OUR WILL TO ALLAH ALMIGHTY. WITHOUT NIYATH A ACTION DID NOT BECOME IBADATH EAVEN IT DONE BY PROPER WAY.

IF WE HAVE PROPER NIYATH OUR OTHER ALL GOOD ACTIONS INCLUDING GOOD RELIGIOUS TRADITION ACTIONS, SOCIAL INTERACTIONS, BUSSINESSES ARE BECOME INFORMAL IBADATHS. WITH GOOD EFFORT AND NIYATH WE CAN POSSIBLE TO MAKE ALL OUR LIFE AS IBADATH TO GOD ALMIGHTY. WE HAVE PROPER RULES FOR FORMAL IBADATHS BY RELIGIOUSLY, BUT WE DO NOT HAVE COMPLETE RULE FOR ALL INFORMAL IBADATHS.

ACTUALLY WE HAVE ISLAMIC PRINCIPLES FOR INFORMAL IBADATH. THAT ARE SUBMITTING OUR WILL TO GOD ALMIGHTY BY PLEDGED THE NIYATH AND DO THE REQUIRED ACTION WITHOUT HARME ANY ONE AND SHOULD KEEP AWAY FROM HARAM (ISLAM PROHIBITED THINGS AND ACTIONS).

PLANTING A TREE WITH THE NIYATH OF ALLAH ALMIGHTYS LIKENESS FOR THE PURPOSE OF HUMAN BEINGS AND ENVIRONMENTS BENEFIT. IS AN EXAMPLE OF INFORMAL IBADATH.

AS PER ISLAM ALL THINGS AND ACTIVITIESE ARE CLASSIFIED AS THREE CATAGORYS ON THE BASIS OF BAD AND

GOOD. THAT ARE HARAM(PROHIBITED) HALAL(ALLOWED) AND UNSPECIFIED. THE FIRST TWO HAVE CLEAR DEFENITIONS AND CLARITIESE, THE THIRD ONE IS THE COMPARITIEVELY BIGGER SECTION MOST OF THEM ARE RELATIEVELY GOOD OR BAD ACCORDING TO SITUATIONS.
 I WILL GIVE SOME EXAMPLES

EXAMPLE 1:
POLICE JAILED A MAN FOR SOME VALID REASON - GOOD THING
PEOPLES JAILED A MAN AND NOT HANDOVER HIM TO POLICE - BAD THING
EXAMPLE 2:
BATHING INSIDE THE BATHROOM - GOOD THING
BATHING ON THE ROAD - BAD THING
EXAMPLE 3:
MARRYING OTHERS UN-MARRIED COUSIN AS PER MUTUAL UNDERSTANDING - GOOD THING
MARRYING OUR UN-MARRIED COUSIN AS PER MUTUAL UNDERSTANDING - BAD THING

SO THE COMBINATION OF FORMAL AND INFORMAL IBADATHS WITH PROPER UNDERSTANDING OF HARAM, HALAL AND UNSPECIFIED SITUATION AND MAKE PROPER DICISIONS AND ACTIONS WITH FULL TIME GOD CONCIOUSNESS MAKE A MAN

MENTALY AND SPIRITUALLY ENLIGHTED
ONE.

CHAPTER-7

PRIMARY AND SECONDARY PURPOSE OF LIFE

YES, I KNOW ALL OF US HAVE SOME ANSWERS. BUT THE ANSWER AND ITS CLARITY MAY VARIES.

AS PER MY UNDERSTANDING THE PRIMARY PURPOUSE OF THIS EARTHLY LIFE IS GETTING ALLAH ALMIGHTYS HOLLY SOUL NEARNESS AND ISHQ (LOVE). I AM CONSIDERED THIS IS AS THE ONLY PURPOUSE OF OUR LIFE.

NOW SOME ONE WILL DEVELOPE A DOUT EVERYTHING IS SUBMITING TO GOD ALMIGHTYS INTEREST AND GOD MONITERING EVERYING. THEN WHAT IS SECONDARY PURPOSE?

AT NORMAL LIFE MOST OF US NOT PRACTICING GOD CONCIOUSNESS IN FULL MEANING AND MAKE EVERY THOUGHT AND ACT AS IBADHATH (GOD LIKED ONE). ACTUALLY THAT IS THE ONLY PURPOUSE OF OUR LIFE. THAT IS THE MOST ADVISIBLE WAY OF PEACE IN THIS LIFE AND SUCCESS IN HEARAFTER.

SO I AM DIVIDING LIFE PURPOSE AS TWO FOR EASY PRACTICING. THE PRIMARY PURPOUSE AND SECONDARY PURPOUSE.

IN PRIMARY PURPOUSE I BEFORE SAID GOD ALMIGHTY NEARNESS AND ISHQ(LOVE) ARE TASK. FOR THAT WE SHOULD MAINTAN GOD CONCIOUSNESS WITH FORMAL IBADATHS OF ISLAM WITH JUSTCE IN OUR EVERY ACTION OF LIFE AND GOOD DEEDS.

MY ADVICE IS FOR GOD ALMIGHTYS REAL NEARNESS IS THE NEXT STEP MAKE ALL OTHER ACTIONS MEANS SECONDARY PURPOUSES MORE TRUTH FULL AND GOOD. MAKE OUR ALL BUSSINESSES, ASSETS, CAPITALS, RELATIONS FREE FROM BAD AND MAKE CONTINOUS PURIFICATION.

MAINTAIN A SUPREAME UNFORM ALL POWER GOD ALMIGHTYS PICTURE WITH A LOCATION OUT SIDE HOLLOW GLOBE ARSH TO INFINITY AND UNFORM GOD ALMIGHTYS HOLLY SOULS PICTURE IN MIND INSIDE THE ARSH, AND SUBMITT YOUR WILL TO GOD ALMIGHTY WITH THE TRUE UNDERSTANDING OF GOD IS REAL, AND PURIFY YOUR LIFE FROM ALL BAD ACTIONS, READ AND THINK ABOUT THE QURAAN BY UNDERSTANDING ITS MEANING AND TRANSFORM ALL YOUR ACTS TO ACTS OF VIRTUE. ALL THESE WILL LEADS TO GOD ALMIGHTYS ISHQ(LOVE) AND NEARNESS, IF GOD WISHES.

SOME ONE WILL DOUT WHAT IS MEAN BY GOD ALMIGHTYS NEARNESS, IT HAVE ANY PHYSICAL OR BIOLOGYCAL EFFECT? YES, IN THAT STAGE ALLAHS HOLLY SOUL WILL MAKE RELATION WITH YOU. HOLLY SOUL WILL HEAL YOU AND GUIDE YOU. THAT IS THE SUPREAM STATE WE CAN ACHIEVE IN THIS EARTHLY LIFE. NOTHING HAVE MORE VALUE THAN THAT.

IF ALLAH ALMIGHTY LIKE US IN SUCH A WAY, OUR SUCCESS IN HEAR AFTER ALSO 100% GUARANTY. SO THE REAL PURPOUSE OF OUR EACH ACT AND LIFE SHOULD BE GOD ALMIGHTYS LIKENESS THAT WILL LEAD US TO GOD ALMIGTHYS NEARNESS.

NOW A QUESTION WILL ARISES, FROM WHERE WE WILL GET THE KNOWLEDGE OF GOD LIKED THINGS? I WILL SAY FROM QURAN AND YOUR SOUL AND GOOD ISLAMIC TRADITIONS.

CHAPTER-8

94

TWO QUALITIES REQUIRED FOR COMPLETING A TASK

IF WE SEARCHING SOME ONE FOR DOING OUR SOME TASK. WE WILL TAKE A INTERVIEW OF THEM FIRST. FOR WHAT? FOR CHECKING THEIR CAPABILITIES TO PERFORM SUCH TASK AND IF IT IS OKAY, WE CAN INVITE THEM TO DO THAT WORK.

MY SUBJECT IS ALSO SAME BUT I CLASSIFYING ENTAIRE QUALITIESE AS TWO CATOGARY. BOTH ARE EQUALY IMPORTANT, ABSENCE OF ONE CATOGARY QUALITY LEADS THE PERSON IS IN CAPABLE FOR DOING THAT TASK OR A BAD ONE FOR THE TASK ASINNED ORGANIZATION. WE WILL GET CLEAR LIGHT ABOUT THIS SUBJECT FROM PROPHET MOSES HISTORY.

TWO QUALITIES ARE

HE OR SHE IS A TRUST WORTHY TO THE TASK ASSINED PERSON OR GROUP

HE OR SHE SHOULD BE CAPABLE IN ALL MEANS TO PERFORM THE TASK

I AM A MECHANICAL ENGINEER BY CARRIER, FROM MY OBSERVATIONS OF SO MEANY COLLEAGUES AND EMPLOYEES. I UNDERSTAND ONE THING, FROM THIS TWO CATEGORY OF QUALITYS MEANY PEOPLE LACING ANY ONE OF THE TWO QUALITIESE.

SOME OF THEM KNOWNS HOW TO PERFORM THE TASK BUT NOT TRUST WORTHY TO THE ORGANIZATION. BUT THEY WILL SURVIVE THEIR BECAUSE THEY KNOW HOW TO PERFORM THE TASK. SAME TIME SOME OF THEM ARE TRUST WORTHY TO THE

ORGANIZATION BUT DO NOT HAVE CLEAR UNDERSTANDING ABOUT HOW TO PERFORM THE TASK, I AM NOT TELLING ABOUT THE NEW JOINES. IF A PERSON IS TRUST WORTHY AND A KEEN SEEKER WE CAN POSSIBLE TO DEVELOP THEM FOR THE ORGANIZATION. BUT THE FIRST CASE PROPER MONITERING IS THE ONLY SOLUTION.

CHAPTER-9

SCIENCE AND RELIGION

SCIENCE IS SCINCE BECAUSE OF ITS WAY OF AQURING KNOWLEDGE AND INVENSIONS. THE BASIC WORKING PRINCIPLE OF SCIENCE IS SCECPTISM AND RATIONALISM NOT NON-RELIGIOUSNESS.

A THEORY LEVEL SCIENTIST SHOULD MAINTAIN A HABIT OF SCEPTISM AND RATIONALISM. INVENSIONAL LEVEL SCIENTIST IS MORE USING RATIONALISM AND COMMON SENSE.

BOTH SHOULD MAINTAINING UPDATED KNOWLEDGE OF THEIR GENERATION. WITH OUT UPDATED KNOWLEDGE IT IS DIFFICULT TO RE CHECK THE KNOWLEDGE AQURED THROUGH SCIENTIFIC WAY OR MOVE FORWARD ON SCIENTIFIC WAY. BEFORE MILLANIOUMS KNOWLEDGE IS LIMITED THAT IS WHY MORE SCHOLERS PRACTICED AS POLYMATHS. NOW A DAYS CONCENTRATION TO ANY FILD BECOME TREND BECAUSE OF WAST MEGORITY OF KNOWLEDGE IN DIFFERENT BRANCHES. THIS TREND HAVE GOOD AND BAD SIDE ALSO. THE GOOD ONE IS THE PERSON BECOME PROMINENT IN ANY AREA VERY FASTLY THE BAD SIDE IS HE OR SHE CAN NOT GET WHOLE IDEA.

SCIENCE AS A METHODOLOGY OF AQUARING KNOWLEDGE AS MORE THAN A KNOWLEDGE LIBRARY.

THAT IS WHY ONE GENERATIONS SCIENTIFIC THEORYS SOME TIMES BECOME FALLS

WHEN SCIENTIST RE-THEORISED IT BY SCEPTISM AND RATIONALISM WITH MORE UPDATED KNOWLEDGE. IT IS THE SPECIALITY OF SCIENTIFIC METHODOLOGY. THAT IS WHY I CALLED SCIENCE IS A METHODOLOGY OR WAY MORE THAN A PERMANENT KNOWLEDGE LIBRARY. PARADISE SHIFT IS THE SPECIALITY OF SCIENCE THAT IS NOT POSSIBLE IN RELIGION BECAUSE ITS BASIC SOURCE ARE NOT RELATED TO INVENTION BUT MORE RELATED TO SPIRITUAL REVELATIONS FROM GOD. BUT CHANGES HAPPENDS BECAUE HUMAN INTEREPTION. ACTUALLY ONLY REFRESHING AND UPDATION IS POSSIBLE IN A TRUE RELIGION OTHER WISE THAT IS NOT A RELIGION. THAT IS A INVENSION. I KNOW SOME RELIGIONS CLAIMS THAT IS A INVENTED ONE.

I WILL SAY A SCIENTIST SHOULD AQURE UPDATED KNOWLEDGE BUT DON NOT BELIEVE 100% IN THEM, I CAN SAY THEORY BASIS WE ACHIVE A GREAT LEVEL NOT 100% BUT GOOD. THEIR ALSO POSSIBILITYS OF IMPROOVEMENTS AND CORRUCTION. IN THAT WAY WE WILL GO FORWARD WE WILL UNDERSTAND THE HUMAN POSSIBLE LEVEL OF KNOWLEDGE ABOUT THIS UNIVERSE, BUT NOT GOD. IF GOD WISHES WE CAN SEE GOD. BUT THAT IS A DISTANCE REALITY IN THIS EARTHLY LIFE. BUT WE CAN

SPIRITUALY CONNECT WITH GOD ALMIGHTY.

PROOVED SCIENTIFIC UNDERSTANDING OF ALL THING ARE 100% REALITY SO FAR, I WILL SAY SOME ARE NOT 100%, I WILL GIVE AN EXAMPLE;

SUBJECT IS NATURE OF LIGHT, WE ALL KNOW WE STUDIED IT IN SCHOOL CLASSESS NOW MORE UPDATED ARE AVAILABLE I WILL STICK ON THE BASIC INTERPRETATION

I WILL SAY SCIENTIST NOT REALLY EXPLAINED THE REAL CHARACTER OF LIGHT, BUT THEY IDENTIFIED SOME QUALITIESE AND EXPLAINE IT BY SYMBOLISATION.

FIRST A THEORY IS ARISED WHICH STATES THAT LIGHT HAVE PARTICLE NATURE. THEY EXPLAYED ALL CHARECTERISTICS ON THAT WAY. LATER THEY UNDERSTOOD THAT IT IS NOT POSSIBLE TO EXPLAIN SOME OTHER QUALITIES WITH THIS THEORY.

THEN WAVE CHARECTERISTIC THEORY ARISED AND THEY REJECTED THE FIRST ONE. THEY TRY TO EXPLAIN ALL CHARECTERISTIC THROUGH THAT THEORY, AGAIN THEY FAILED THAT.

THEN THE DUAL CHARECTERISTIC THERY ARISE ACCORDING TO THAT LIGHT HAVE BOTH PARTICLE AND WAVE NATURE. MOST OF THE SCIENTIST SATISFIED AT THAT THEORY. STORY NOT ENDED. WE

UNDERSTANDED IS THE SOME OF THE POSSIBLE UNDERSTANDING OF THAT TIME.

ISAAC NEWTONS THEORY AND INVENSIONS ARE THE MOST REASONABLE ANSWER OF THAT TIME, WHEN EINSTEENS THEORY ARISES EINSTEENS VIEW BECOME MORE PROMINENT ACCORDING TO SCIENTIST. UNLIKE RELIGIOUS PERSONS SCIENTIST KNOWS HOW ITS HAPPENDS, THEIR WAY OF KNOWLEDGE APPROACH IS BOTTOM TO TOP. RELIGIOUS WAY OF KNOWLEDGE APPROACH IS TOP TO BOTTOM, I MEAN GOD TO EARTH APPROACH IN RELIGION AND SURROUNDING TO UNIVERSE APPROACH IN SCIENCE. THAT MAKE THE MOST PROMINENT DIFFERENCE BETWEEN RELIGION AND SCIENCE.

I AM SYMBOLISING RELIGION AS A LESS SUNNY DAY AND COOL NIGHT. SCIENCE AS A SUNNY DAY. NIGHT IS VERY BEATYFULL AS LIKE DAY. IF YOU ONLY FOLLOW SCIENCE YOUR 24 HOURS IS SUNNY DAY. IF YOU WISH YOU WILL GET MOST CLEAR VIEW OF YOUR SURROUNDINGS AT YOUR WHOLE DAY SCINTIFIC VIEW LIFE. SAME TIME YOU WILL MISS SOMETHING, THE VIEW OF BIGGER WORLD, THE KNOWLEDGE OF STARS AND GALAXYS MEANS THE KNOWLEDGE MORE RELATED TO HIGHER KNOWLEDGE. THAT IS DIRECTLY AND RESONABILY EASILY ONLY POSSIBLE THROUGH SYMBOLYC RILIGIOUS NIGHT. SO SYMBOL OF A TRUE RELIGION IS A CLEAR SKY NIGHT AND SHAIDED DAY.

WE HUMANS NEED OUR BOTH LIGHTS THE SCIENCE AND TRUE RELIGION.
I WILL TELL SOME GENERAL POINTS ABOUT RELIGION
I AM CATEGARISING RELIGION AS TWO CATEGORY.
CLAIMING THAT FROM GOD ALMIGHTY
CLAIMING THAT HUMAN INVENSION

MY ADVICE IS CHOICE IS YOURS, SOME RELIGIOUS BODYS CLAIM IS THAT THEIR RELIGION IS THEIR ANCESTERS INVENSION BUT REALITY MAY DIFFER, SAME TIME SOME RELIGIOUS BODYS CLAIMS THAT THEIR RELIGION IS FROM GOD BUT REALITY MAY DIFFER. I AM SURE THIS BOOK WILL GIVE YOU ANSWER.

CHAPTER-10

103

CAPITAL

WE ALL HEARD ABOUT CAPITAL, WHAT IS IT FINANCE ONLY?
MY ANSWER IS NO.
EVERY PERSON HAVE DIFFERENT TYPE OF CAPITALS WITH HIM OR HER, BUT ITS PROPORTION, QUALITY AND QUANTITY VARIESE.
ACTUALLY IT IS CONSIDERED AS THE UTILISABLE STRENTH AND ASSET WE OWN IN OUR CONTROL;
I AM CLASSIFYING MAINLY IT AS

HEALTH CAPITAL
KNOWLEDGE CAPITAL
FINANCE CAPITAL
TIME CAPITAL
CULTURAL CAPITAL

HEALH CAPITAL: GOOD BODY SOUL AND MENTAL STATE IS REQUIRED FOR A PERSONS SUCCESSFUL SURVIVAL AND ACHIEVEMENTS IN EARTHLY LIFE.
AS LIKE A PERSON EACH COUNTRYS SHOULD MAINTAIN SUCH HEALTHY STATE IN THEIR NATION.

KNOWLEDGE CAPITAL: A PERSON WITH GOOD KNOWLEDGE AND IT'S SUCCESSFUL APPLICATION IN HIS OR HER LIFE GIVE THEM THE REAL IDENTITY.
ACHIEVE DEEP KNOWLEDGE AT LEAST IN ONE SUBJECT. THAT IS LIKE WE DIGGING A

WELL IN DEPTH, AT MORE DEPTH CHANCE OF GETTING WATER IS MORE OTHER THAN FLATTER DIGGING WITH SAME EFFORT AND TIME. SAME TIME KEEP GENERAL AWARENESS AND BASIC KNOWLEDGE ABOUT EVERY THING.

A COUNTRYS GOOD HIGHER EDUCATION SYSTEM WITH GOOD QUALITY EDUCATION FROM LOWER SCHOOL CLASSESS AND A RESERVE OF RESERCH KNOWLEDGE ARE TO BE COUNSIDERED AS THAT COUNTRYS CAPITAL.

FINANCE CAPITAL: WE ALL KNOW ABOUT FINANCE CAPITAL AND IT'S IMPORTANCE, IS ANY SPECIFIC MINIMUM LIMIT FOR THAT? MY ANSWER IS IT IS DEPENDS UP ON US AND OUR COUNTRY'S LIVING EXPENSES.

BUT I CAN TELL YOU SOME COMMON THINGS WE SHOULD PRACTICE

ALWAYS KEEP 6 MONTH LIVING EXPENSES AS RESERVE EMERGENCY FUND IN EASILY ACCESSIBLE FORM

DO NOT PUT ALL SAVINGS AND INVESTMENT IN ONE SECTOR

ALL WAYS MAINTAIN LIQUIDITY IN YOUR 50% WEALTH

TRY TO BUY MORE ASSETS WHICH GENERATE GREAT INCOMES AND LESS LIABILITIESE (EG: LOT OF PRIVET CARS) WHICH LEADS TO FINACIAL LOSESS

WHETHER YOU ARE A EMPLOYE, BUSSINESS MAN OR INVESTER DON'T MAKE ANY FINANCIAL SUDDEN STOPE OR START IN ANY SECTOR WITH OUT DO SOME OBSERVATIONS AND WORKOUTS.

FOR NATIONS I KNOW AS LIKE INDIVITUAL SURVIVAL OF THE FITTEST AND ACHIEVERS ARE THE TOPPEST ARE THE REAL PRACTICE. FOR THAT DO BETTER FINANCIAL PLANING, IMPROVE EDUCATION SYSTEM, UTILISE RESOURSES WISELY AND CLEVERLY. IMPROVE NATIONALISM, MAINTAIN GOOD FORIGN RELATIONS AND TRADE, PREVENT CORRUPTION FROM ALL GOVERNMENT BODYS, NOT GIVE MORE THAN 30% RESERATION IN ANY WHERE, THE BASE OF RESERVATION SHOULD BE REGION, FINANCE STATE AND DISEBILITIESE. MAINTAIN A NATIONAL UNIFICATION POLICY WITH EVERY SUB-CULTURE TRADITIONS THEIR SPACE OF FREEDOM. ONE NATION ONE LAW POLICY. IF WE GRATUALY SUCCEDE IN THE IMPLIMENTATION OF THESE POINTS THE NATIONS FUTURE BECOME BRIGHT.

TIME CAPITAL: THIS IS THE ONLY CAPITAL EQUALY AVAILABLE FOR WE ALL. WHO WILL USE IT WISELY HE OR SHE WILL WIN HIS OR HER LIFE. WHO WILL USE IT CARELESSLY HE OR SHE HAVE THE MORE CHANCE TO FAIL.

AS I DISCUSSED IN A EARLY CHAPTER GOD ALMIGHTY HAS ONLY COMPLETE TIME. WE ALL ARE HAVE INCOMPLETE TIME. A QUSTION WILL ARISE WHAT IS TIME? TIME IS THE LIFE TIME OR EXISTING PERIOD OF A LIVING THING OR NON-LIVING THING AND GOD ALMIGHTY. WE ALL HAVE BEGINNING THAT WHY I CALLED OUR SELF AS INCOMPLETE TIME LIVING ORGANISM.

SOME LIVING AND NON –LIVING THINGS HAVE PERMANENT END ALSO. SO THAT KIND THINGS OR ORGANISMS BECOME LIMITED TIME THINGS OR LIVING ORGANISM. TIME IS ACTULLY INFINITE. BECAUSE GOD ALMIGHTY EXISTING IN INFINITY.

WE CAN USE A MECHANICAL CLOCK TO COUNT TIME MECHANICALLY. LIKE WISE SOME OTHER PRINCIPLES WE CAN UTILISE FOR TIME COUNTING. SO COUNTING IS ANOTHER MATTER TIME IS ANOTHER MATTER. WE ALL KNOW DAY AND NIGHT COUNTING BECAUSE OF NATURE AMBEANCE CHANGE. THAT IS A EARTHLY TIME COUNTING METHODE THAT DID NOT MEAN THAT TIME IS MOTION. WITH OUT MOTION ALSO TIME IS TIME. REAL TIME IS GOD ALMIGHTYS TIME THAT IS INFINITE WHETHER GOD MOVES OR NOT, WE CREATIONS EXIST OR NOT. THE REMAINING ARE COUNTING METHODS FOR INCOMPLETE TIME OR LIMITED TIME LIVING THINGS AND NON-LIVING THINGS.

IS TIME HAVE ANY DIRECTION? YES TIME HAVE DIRECTION FOR US MEANS CREATIONS BUT NOT FOR GOD ALMIGHTY. TIME TRAVEL IS NOT POSSIBLE FOR US AND NOT NORMALLY POSSIBLE FOR GOD ALMIGHTY IN CREATIONS CASE. OTHER VISE RE CREATION IS REQUIRED AT PASSED CREATIONS TIME, THAT IS ONLY POSSIBLE IN ALL MEANS BY GOD ALMIGHTY. WE CAN ONLY POSSIBLE IS SPEED TRAVEL TO THE FUTURE DESTINATION.

WE CAN SYMBOLISE CREATIONS TIMING AS A BEGINED AND NON ENDED STRAIGHT LINE IN SUCH TIME LINE OUR HUMAN LIFE STARTED AT SOME POINTS AND IT WILL END AT SOME POINT AT EARTH AND IF WE WILL GET ETERNAL LIFE WE WILL LIVE UP TO INFINITY, IF GOD WISHES.

NOW WE CAN DISCUSS SOME PERSONAL LIFE TIME MATTERS. SUPPOSE A PERSON LIVE UP TO 100 YEARS. FIRST 25 YEARS IS THE MOST IMPORTANT STAGE. WE CAN CONSIDER THIS TIME AS HUMAN DEVELOPMENT STAGE. WE KNOW MOST OF THIS AGES WE ARE NOT FULLY CAPABLE FOR A INDIVITUALY LEADING LIFE. SO SUPPORT FROM FAMILY IS SO IMPORTANT IN THIS STAGE. PARENTS SHOULD BE RESPONSIBLE FOR THE DEVELOPMENT OF THEIR CHILDRENS, BUT AFTER 10 YEAR CONSIDER THEIR INTERESTS ALSO. IT IS BETTER TO START SCHOOLING AT AGE OF 8.

BEFORE THAT WE CAN TEACH THEM. IF THEY WANT WE CAN SEND AT PLAY SCHOOL WHICH INCLUDES CRICKET, FOOT BALL AND BASE BALL LIKE TEAM GAMES.

IN THIS STAGE SHOULD PRACTICE SOME SPORTS GAMES THAT WILL HELPS THEM FOR BULDING A STRONG BODY AND MIND. I HAVE AN ADVICE FOR EDUCATION AUTHORITYS, IN A WEEKLY SCHEDULE SPEND 40% OF TOTAL TIME FOR PRACTICING ART PROGRAMS AND SPORTS GAMES.

ADD COLLEAGE LEVEL SUBJECTS BASICS TO SCHOOLING SYSTEM. MECHANICAL BASICS, ELECTRICAL AND ELECTRONICS BASICS AND IT KNOWLEDGE IN SCHOOL EDUCATION. TEACH RULES AND REGULATIONS OF THE NATION. TEACH INTERPERSON RELATIONSHIP MANNERS. ETC.

MORE THAN HALF OF THE HUMANS ARE NATURALLY MORE INTERESTED IN ART SUBJECTS THAN SCIENCE AND TECHNOLOGY. SO TEACHING THESE SUBJECTS FROM THE SCHOOL LEVEL WILL HELPS EVERY ONE TO NOTICE THIS PART OF OUR KNOWLEDGE ALSO.

I AM NOT EXCLUDING OTHER SUBJECTS I AM ADVICING TO MAINTAIN OR INCLUDE THIS ALSO. SOMEBODY WILL ASK WHY I AM NOT ADVICING ACCOUNTING AND COMMERCE IN SCHOOL CLASSES, YAH, I AM FORGOTTEN, THAT IS ALSO A MOST

ADVISABLE ONE, AND ALL THESE EDUCATIONS ARE COMMON FOR ALL GENDER.

FATHER AND MOTHER SHOULD INTRODUCE THEIR CHILD TO EVERY PART OF THE SOCIETY. INDIRECTLY LEAD THEM FOR MAKING AND MAINTAINING RELATIONS. TEACH GOOD FAMILY VALUES AND RELATIONSHIP ETHICS.

ACT AS A COACH AND NOT AS ADMINISTRATOR. SUPPORT THEM MINIMUM UP TO THEIR CARRIER STARTING.

I AM SURE IF A FAMILY PASS THIS STAGE SUCCESSFULLY THEY SUCCEDED THEIR LIFE MORE THAN 50%

FROM 25 TO 65 WE CAN CONSIDER AS THE NEXT STAGE OR ACHIEVEMENT STAGE. ACTUALLY THIS IS OUR EXPANSION STAGE BY OUR CONCIOUS EFFORTS. IF WE CARELESS ABOUT THIS STAGE WE CAN NOT EXPAND OUR PERSONALITY TO SOCIETY OR CAN NOT ACHIEVE MORE SUCCESS AND PEACE IN LIFE.

THIS IS THE TIME FOR CARRIER AND BUSINESS ESTABLISHMENTS. THIS IS THE BETTER TIME FOR START A NEW STAGE OF PERSONAL LIFE, THE MARRIAGE LIFE. AS PER MY UNDERSTANDING A MARRIAGE RELATION SHOULD START WITH FORMAL PROCEDURE, AND MAINTAN WITH MUTUAL LOVE, UNDERSTANDING, TRUST AND GOOD VALUES, MUTUAL CONSIDERATION,

SUBMITTING MUTUALLY, MUTUAL CARING, FRENDSHIP AND FREEDOM.

I AM NOT PROMOTING ANY KIND OF MEN AND WOMEN INTIMACY RELATION WITHOUT MARRIAGE OTHER THAN NORMAL FAMILY RELATIONS BETWEEN MUTUALLY WELL KNOWN PERSONS. IF REQUIRED, I AM NOT AGAINST FRIENDS SHIP LOVE BUT TRY OR APPLICABLE ONLY IF YOU BOTH ARE NOT IN MARRIAGE RELATION. JUST CONSIDER FRIEDS SHIP LOVE AS A BEGINING OF MARRIAGE AND NOT AS MARRIAGE. AND THE AIM OF FRIENDS SHIP LOVE SHOULD BE MARRIAGE LOVE LIFE. IF YOU DON NOT HAVE SUCH DREAMS DO NOT MAKE A GIRL FRIEND OR BOY FRIEND LOVE RELATION. SAME GENDER MARRIAGE IS A BAD IDEA, SO THE COUPLE SHOULD BE OPPOSITE GENDER, THAT IS ALSO VERY IMPORTANT.

AND WHAT ABOUT AGE? ANY PERSON OF THIS STAGES AGE RAGE CAN MARRY ANY OTHER PERSON OF THIS STAGES AGE RANGE, BUT + OR – TEN YEARS IS THE BEST CHOICE. ALL AGES OF THIS STAGE ARE RELATED TO PERSONS MENTAL AND SOUL STATE MORE THAN NORMAL PHYSICAL.

ANOTHER QUESTION WILL ARISE HOW MEANY MARRIAGES WE CAN DO, MY ANSWER IS ITS DEPENDS UP TO YOU, BUT AT A TIME MAXIMUM 2 FOR MEN AND 1 FOR WOMEN. WHAT IS THE MOST ADVISABLE STYLE?

THAT ALL WE KNOW SINGLE MARRIAGE FOR A LIFE TIME IS THE GOOD ONE. IF ONE PERSON DO NOT WANT TO MARRY BECAUSE HE OR SHE DO NOT WANT SEXUAL LIFE AND A COUPLE LIFE, THAT IS ALSO OKAY. BUT, IF THEY WANT BOTH THEY SHOULD MARRY.

IF MEN WANT ONE MORE MARRIAGE WITH THE SAME TIME HE SHOULD TAKE WRITTEN PERMISSION FROM HIS FIRST WIFE OR CURRENT WIFE WITH TWO WITNESSESS ONE FROM WIFE'S FAMILY AND ONE FROM HIS FAMILY. THEN SUBMIT IT TO THE GOVERNMENT AUTHORITY TO GET APPROVAL FOR THE SECOND MARRIAGE. I KNOW MOST OF THE NATIONS HAVE THEIR ON LAW. I AM TELLING ABOUT THE RELIGIOUS LAW UNDER THE CORE OF ADAMIC RELIGIONS WITH LATEST UPDATE.

I BEFORE TOLD THAT MARRIAGE LIFE SHOULD START WITH FORMAL PROCEDURE, HOW IS IT? I WILL GIVE A BRIEF EXPLANATION. IT SHOULD BE A WRITTEN CONTRACT BETWEEN TWO PERSONS WHO WISHES TO MARRY. THE GOVEMENT OF NATION SHOULD BE THE AUTHORITY OF APROVAL AND COUPLES ARE THE PRACTITIONERS OF THE MARRIAGE CONTACT. MINIMUM 4 PERSON SHOULD SIGN IN THE CONTRACT AS WITNESS 2 FROM WOMENS SIDE AND 2 FROM MENS SIDE. ONES THE CONTRACT WILL ESTABLISHED

WITH IN 3 MONTHS IT SHOULD NOT BE POSSIBLE TO INVALIDATE.

FOR INVALIDATING THE CONTRACT WRITTEN APPLICATION SHOULD BE SUBMITTED TO GOVERNMENT AUTHORITYS. WITHOUT WRITTEN INVALIDATING APPLICATION TO THE GOVERNMENT AUTHORITY THE MARRIAGE WILL NOT CONSIDER FOR INVALIDATION, IF THERE IS A GOVERNMENT. ORAL COMMUNICATION IS NOT ENOUGH FOR INVALIDATING A WRITTEN CONTRACT.

IF THERE IS NO GOVERNMENT FAMILISE OF BOTH MEN AND WOMEN ARE SUFFICIENT FOR MAKING THE RELATION CONTRACT AND ITS WITHDRAWEL, MEANS IT WILL BECOME A PERSONAL MATTER. AFTER 3 MONTHS IT IS POSSIBLE BY MUTUAL AGREED OR INDIVITUAL WIDRAWAL. FINANCIAL OR ASSET TRANSACTION IS FOR ONE PARTYS BENEFIT IS NOT REQUIRED BEFORE CONTRACT OR AFTER CONTRACT. ONES THE MARRIGE CONTRACT IS INVALIDATED IT SHOULD NOT BE POSSIBLE FOR BOTH OF THEM A NEXT MARRIAGE WITH IN 3 MONTHS. IT IS POSSIBLE FOR BOTH OF THEM TO AGAIN RE-MARRIAGE WITH IN THREE MONTHS AFTER MARRIAGE CONTRACT INVALIDATION BUT BETWEEN BOTH OF THEM, NOT TO OTHERS, IF THEY WISHES. ANY TRADITIONAL RITUALS IS NOT REQUIRED FOR ACTUAL RELIGIOUS

MARRIAGE, THE RITUALS ARE MORE RELATED TO CULTURE THAN RELIGION.

NOW WE WILL THINK WHAT WILL BE THE CONDITIONS IN THE MARRIAGE CONTRACT. MOST OF THE CONDITIONS AND COUPLE RELATION PRACTISES ARE I EXPLAINED. SO WE CAN PLACE THAT ARE IN THE CORE OF THE CONTRACT. IF BOTH COUPLES AND THEIR FAMILY WANT ADDITIONAL CONDITIONS THEY CAN ADD IT TO THE CONTRACT BUT IT SHOULD BE WITH IN GOOD TRADITION AND VALUES OF HUMANS. ONE MORE IMPORTANT THING IF COUPLES INVALIDATING THEIR CONTRACT AND THEY HAVE CHILDRENS IN THAT RELATIONSHIP AND THEIR AGE IS BELOW 25 THE FATHER OF THE CHILDREN IS RESPONSIBLE FOR THEIR LIVING EXPENSES UP TO 25 YEARS. IF THE MOTHER AND CHILDREN WANTS THAT.

SO MARRIAGE IS THE ONLY THING IN THIS STAGE? NOT ONLY, BUT A SUCCESSFUL FAMILY LIFE IS ONE OF THE MOST IMPORTANT THING THROUGH THE ENTIRE LIFE. SO SPEND OUR VALUABLE TIME WITH FAMILY. CREATE GREAT MEMORYS AT EACH STAGES OF LIFE. IF WE DO NOT HAVE SUCH MEMORYS AT THIS STAGE. AFTER 65 YEARS WE WILL FACE SOME PROBLEMS. OTHER THINGS ARE, IF WE DON'T HAVE CARIER OR SOCIAL SUCCESS IN 2 ND STAGE OF LIFE WE WILL REALLY FACE SOME PROBLEMS IN OUR SETTLEMENT STAGE THE THIRD AND FINAL

STAGE. THAT WILL AFFECT OUR SELF RESPECT AND SELF CONFIDENT. IN THAT STAGE WE WILL UNDERSTOOD THAT WHERE OUR SCHOOL FRIENDS AND COLLEAGES REACHED AND NOW WE DO NOT HAVE ENERGY OR SURROUNDING CHARISMATIC AMBIANCE FOR A STRONG MOVE. A PERSON SUCCEDE IN THE DEVELOPMENT STAGE AND EXPANSION STAGE CONTINOUES THEIR SUCCESS IN SETTLEMENT STAGE ALSO.

SOME BODY WILL TELL THESE ALL ABOUT THE MATTER OF DHUNIYA(WORLD) WE ONLY WISHES GOD ALMIGHTYS SATISFATION AND NEARNESS. IF YOU ARE LIKE THAT STATE MORE THAN ANYTHING AT ANY STAGE AND ANY CONDITION I AM ALSO WITH YOU. BUT MOST OF THEM FAILING THEIR ALSO IN THE ABSENCE OF A SUFFICIENT LIFE, THAT IS THE REALITY.

AND IT IS ALSO POSSIBLE TO GET GOD ALMIGHTYS NEARNESS AND SATISFACTION WITH A RICH FLAVOURED LIFE IF WE HAVE THAQWA (CLEAR UNDERSTANDIND OF GOOD(HALAL), BAD(HARAM), UNCOFIRMED THINGS AND ITS PROPER PRACTICE IN LIFE WITH GOD CONCIOUSNESS). WE KNOW KALIFA ABUBAKAR, KALIFA UMER AND SOME OF THE GREAT SAHABAS ARE COMPARITIVELY GOOD AT THEIR WELTH ALSO.

NOW I WILL DISCUSS SOMETHING ABOUT CHARACTER BUILD UP. IT IS A GOOD THING

TO MAINTAIN HOBYS AS A PART OF LIFE TIME. GOOD SOCIAL MEDIA CONTENT CREATION, BOOK READING AND WRITING, STOCK MARKET OBSERVATON AND INVESTING ARE SOME OF THE EXAMPLES OF GOOD HOBYS WE CAN MAINTAN. IT WILL HELP US IN SOUL WISDOM, MIND POWER AND SOCIAL SUCCESS, IF WE UTILICE IT IN A PROPER WAY.

ANOTHER ADVISABLE THING IS MAINTAIN A TRAVEL AND JOURNEY HABIT. LIKE DESTINATION TRAVEL BIRDS EVERY YEAR ONE OR TWO MONTHS SPEND FOR TRAVELLING TO ANOTHER WORLD OF LANDS. MAKE A RELATION WITH ANOTHER CULTURES THROUGH TRAVELLING. AMONGS FROM SUCH EXPERIENCE SELECT SOME SPECIFIC CONTRY AND PLACES AS OUR REGULAR VISITING PLACES. BUILD RELATION WITH PEOPLES OF SUCH LANDS AND BECOME FRIENDS. EVERY YEAR SPEND SOME TIME IN SUCH LANDS AND REFRESH OUR RELATIONSHIP WITH FRIEDS OF THAT PLACES. WE CAN GO THEIR WITH OUR FAMILY, IF WE WISHES. IF IT IS POSSIBLE BUY A HOME THEIR. THAT TIME WE BECOME A MAN OF RELATIVELY MORE INTERNATIONAL. ACTUALLY I AM A SUPPORTER OF DUAL COUNTRY CITICENSHIP. THAT IS A GOOD THING FOR BOTH PERSON AND COUNTRY. BUT THE NATION SIDE BOTH COUNTRY SHOULD

MAINTAIN LEAGAL TIE-UP AND LEAGAL CIMILARITIES, FOR PERSONS SIDE THAT IS ALSO A GOOD THING.

SO TIME TRAVEL IS POSSIBLE FOR OUR SOUL BY REMEMBERING OR ASSUMING OR WITH GOD ALMIGHTYS DIRECTION BUT NOT THROUGH OUR BODY BY GOING THEIR. SO A TRAVELLER OF GREAT DESTINATIONS WITH INTERWELLS WILL BE GOOD TIME TRAVELLER BY SOUL ALSO.

BETWEEN AGE 30 AND 50 MINIMUM ONE TIME TAKE ONE COMPLETE YEAR BRAKE FROM CARIER AND BUSSINESS AND SPEND THAT TIME COMPLETELY WITH FAMILY. THAT TIME WILL HELP YOU TO THINK AND ASSESS MORE ABOUT YOUR LIFE.

THIS STAGE IS THE BEST TIME TO START PARTICIPATION IN ANY GOOD SOCIAL ORGANIZATION OR SOCIAL MISSION. MOST OF US ARE CITIZENS UNDER DIFFERENT NATIONS, SO PARTICIPATE IN NATION BUILDING AND IMPROVEMENT PROGRAMS.

SO ENJOY EACH TIME AS LIKE DIFFERENT SEASONS. OUR EACH STAGE WILL GIVE DIRECTION FOR OUR NEXT STAGE, SO NEVER LIVE CARELESSLY.

THE PASSED TIME WE WILL NEVER GET SO SPEND IT WITH GREAT EXPERIENCES AND MAKE GOOD MEMORYS FOR FUTURE. OUR EARTHLY MEMORYS WILL RETAIN IN OUR SOUL AFTER OUR DEATH ALSO. SO MAKE GOOD MEMORYS.

SETTLEMENT STAGE IS ALSO A GOOD STAGE IF WE HAVE ACHIEVEMENTS AND GOOD MEMORYS. WE CAN LIVE ACTIVE LIFE IN THIS STAGE UP TO OUR POSSIBLE LEVEL OF LIFE. WE CAN SPEND TIME WITH OUR GRAND CHILDRENS, MAKE FRIENDSHIP WITH THEM.STUDY NEW TECHNOLOGY ADVANCEMENT AND UPDATE THROUGH OUT THE LIFE. SAME AS EACH STAGE SPEND SOME TIME FOR PRAYER AND WORSHIP, SPEND SOME TIME FOR MEDITATION. ACTUALLY OUR AGE INCREASES SAME TIME OUR CAPACITY AND CAPABILITY ALSO INCREASING THROUGH OUR MIND AND SOUL UPDATION BUT IN THE THIRD STAGE BODY STARTED TO BECOME WEAK THAT AFFECT OUR BODY AND MIND. IN THAT STAGE BODY SOUL COMMUNICATION THROUGH MIND STARTING TO BECOME WEAK. THAT WILL REDUCE OUR PHYSICAL CAPABILITYS AND CONCIOUSNESS LEVEL. AT EARTHLY LIFE OUR CONCIOUSNESS IS MOSTLY GETTING THROUGH OUR MIND. AFTER DEATH ONLY SOUL WILL GET ITS FULL CONCIOUSNESS. IF WE LIVE A GOOD BALANCED LIFE WE WILL PASSED THROUGH THIS STAGE ALSO AT GOOD CONDITION.

BALANCED THE LIFE IS THE COMBINATION OF GOOD FOOD HABIT, GOOD SLEEPING, EXERCISE, GOOD LIFE ACHIEVEMENTS AND MAINTAINING GOOD RELATION WITH

FRIENDS, FAMILY AND SOCIETY. THIS WILL HELP US AT EACH STAGES OF OUR LIFE.

DAILY TIMING
AS PER MY CLOCK MORNING 6:00AM IS MY 1: DT-DAY TIME AND EVENING 6:00 PM IS MY 1:00 NT-NIGHT TIME. UP TO 3:00DT MEANS 8:00 AM IN MORNING TIME. IT IS ADVISABLE TO SPEND THIS TIME FOR PRAYER, MEDITATION AND EXERCISE. FROM 3:00 DT TO 12: DT BETTER TIME FOR JOB AND OTHER PRODUCTION ACTIVITIESE. FROM 12:00DT TO 6:00 NT BETTER TIME FOR GOING MARKET. 6:00 NT TO 11:00NT BETTER TIME FOR SLEEPING.
WISHING A GOOD WHOLE DAY.

I WILL GIVE SIMILE ABOUT THE IMPORTANT OF TIME. WE ARE PLAYING A PART OF FOOT BAAL TEAM, AFTER THE FULL TIME. THE GAME OPPOSITE TEAM WIN THE GAME BY 2 GOALS. FANS COME TO ASKING US WHY YOU ARE NOT MAKE EAVEN NOT A ATTENT TO SHOOT A GOAL, A CLEVER MAN FROM MY TEAM SAID THEM, AT THE TIME OF MATCH WE HAVE SO MEANY DIFFICULTIESE AND OPPOSITIONS. SO WE PLANNED TO SHOOT AFTER THE MATCH.
SO, TIME IS IMPORTANT…

CULTURAL CAPITAL: CULTURAL CAPITAL IS MORE SOCIETY BASED CAPITAL. SUPPOSE A

SPECIFIC SOCIETY HAVE A STYLE OF CULTURE, SO THE LEADERS OF THAT SOCITY CAN UNITE THEM THROUH THAT CULTURAL TRENDS. PERSON ALSO CAN BENEFIT IT BY BECOMING PART OF IT. CULTURAL CAPITAL IS A POWER FULL ONE THAT CHANGED THE HISTORY OF SO MEANY NATIONS ALSO. ONE OF THE REASON FOR COLLAPSE OF SOVIET UNION IS THE ACTION OF DIFFERENT CULTURAL CAPITALS OF THEIR SOCIETY.

CHAPTER-11

CULTURE, KILAFATH AND NATIONALISM

WE ALL HAVE DIFFERENT NATURES, FROM ALL THESE NATURES OUR GOOD NATURES ARE CALLED AS CULTURE. SO BECOME A PERSON OR NATION OF GOOD CULTURE DO NOT ACT WITH BAD PART OF OUR NATURE, ACCEPT ALL GOOD THINGS AND ACT WITH OUR GOOD PORSION OF NATURE. SO WHAT WE ARE DOING IS NOT CULTURE ALL WAYS, WHAT WE ARE DOING WITH GOOD INTENSION AND ACTION AND WITH OR WITH OUT ITS TRADITION ARE CALLED CULTURE. IT IS NOT LOCKED IN ANY CENTURY IT IS IN PRECENT AND IT CONTINOUES IN THE FUTURE ALSO. ACTUALLY IT SHOULD MAINTAIN A PROGRESSIVE GROWTH IN OUR PRECENT AND IN THE FUTURE LIFE.

WHY ARE YOU TELLING ABOUT NATIONS? YOU DO NOT KNOW IT IS A SEPERATION FACTOR FROM THE REST OF THE WORLD? I AM TELLING ABOUT THIS BECAUSE IT HAS A UNITING FACTOR ALSO SAME TIME WE NEED SOME COMPETITIONS ALSO, OTHER WISE WE DID NOT ACHIEVE GREAT THINGS, SO NATIONALISM UNDER CULTURE, IDEOLOGY OR ETHNICITY IS THE BEST OPTION. SOMEBODY WILL THINK THAT ARE THE BAD OPTIONS, FINANCE IS BETTER FOR NATIONAL IDENTITY. MY ANSWER IS FINACE IS A UNIVERSAL MATTER AND EVERY ONE CAN NOT MODEL A NATIONS FINANCIAL POLICIESE INSIDE THEIR NATION BECAUSE OF SO MEANY DIFFERENCES.

MY EXPECTATION IS IDEOLOGICAL DIFFERENCES BECOME LESS PROMINENT IN UPCOMING TIME AND CENTURIES. THEN WE WILL HAVE LESS MATTERS FOR NATIONALITY, WE CAN COMPARITIVELY EASILY ADOPT FINANCIAL MODELS BUT EASILY CAN NOT IMPLIMENT BECAUSE OF RESOURCE DIFFERENCE OF EACH NATIONS. CULTURAL AND ETHNICITY MATTER IS DIFFERENT. SAME ETHNICITY PEOPLES MAY PRACTICE DIFFERENT CULTURS, LIKE THAT DIFFERENT ETHNICITY PEOPLES MAY PRACTICE SAME CULTUR. SO ETHNICITY OR CULTURE OR BOTH WILL BE THE BEST OPTION FOR NATIONALISM. WHICH ONE IS THE MOTO OF THE NATION DEPENDS UP ON THE NATIONAL INTEREST

AS WE CONSIDER AS THE SEPERATION FACTOR FROM OUT SIDE NATION. MORE THAN SEPERATION FACTOR IT SHOULD BE IDENTITY FACTOR. BASIS OF NATIONALISM IS INSIDE UNITENESS, OUT SIDE COMMEN RELATIONS AND COMPETION. SO CULTURE AND ETHNICITY OF PEOPLES ARE MORE CONSIDERABLE FACTOR THAN FINANCE AND IDEOLOGY FOR NATION IDENTITY. I KNOW SOME NATIONS HAVE DIFFERENT ETHNIC GROUPS, IN THAT CASE THEY CAN PROMTE CULTURAL IDENTITY OR IF THEY ARE SAME RELIGION, THEY CAN PROMOTE RELIGIOUS IDEOLOGY WITH THE BASIS OF RATIONAL AND SCIENTIFIC THINKING. ANY

NATIONS INSIDE DIFFERENSESS IS LESS AND NATIONALISM IS STRONG MEANS CHANCE OF FLURISHING THAT NATION IS HIGH, OTHER WISE NATION WILL UNDERGOES THROUGH COMPLICATIONS IN ADMINISTRATIONS AND PEACE MAKING.

I HAVE SOME SUJECTIONS FOR ELECTION METHODS FOR SELECTING RULERS FOR SUCH NATIONS

AT FIRST, SET REQUIRED QUALIFICATION FOR EACH POSITIONS. THEN INVITE AND SHORT LIST CANDIDATES AS PER THE QUALIFICATION REQUIREMENT. WE CAN IMPLEMENT THIS METHOD FROM DISTRICT LEVEL TO PRIME MINISTER AND PRECEDENT LEVEL. AMONGS FROM SHORT LISTED CANDIDATES OF MLA'S AND MP'S, ELECTION COMMISION CONDUCT A DRAW ELECTION. WHO WILL WIN THROUGH DRAW BECOME MLA OR MP. THIS MLA'S CAN ELECT MINISTERS AND CHIEF MINISTER OF THE STATE OR PROVINCE. MP'S CAN ELECT CENTRAL MINISTERS AND PRIME MINISTER OF THE NATION. AND BOTH MLA'S AND MP'S SHOULD PARTICIPATE IN THE PREDENT SELECTION ELECTION BY VOTING TO THE SHORTILISTED CANDIDATES. ALL MIMISTERS, CHIEF MINISTERS AND PRIME MINISTER SHOULD SELCT BY THE MLA'S AND MP'S THROUGH VOTING ELECTION FROM THE SHORT LISTED CANDIDATES OF EACH CATEGORY.

I WILL GIVE AN EXAMPLE FOR REQUIRED QUALIFICATION, IN THE CASE OF FINACE MINISTER HE OR SHE SHOULD BE A SUCCESSFUL ENTERPRENUER OR BUSSINESS MAN WITH MINIMUM A DEGREE QUALIFICATION.

ANOTHER A PUBLIC VOTING ELECTION (NOT DRAW ELECTION) ALSO NEED TO CONDUCT FOR THE SELECTION OF VIGILANT GOVERNMENT COMMITY. CIVIL SERVICE CADER CANDIDATED CAN CONDEST IN THIS ELECTION. THIS COMMITY SHOULD BE 30% SIZE OF THE RULING GOVERNMENT MINISTRY, AND WITH CABINET OR MINISTER RANK. THEY SHOULD NOT HAVE DIRECT RULING POWER SAME TIME THEY SHOULD HAVE ALL THE POWER OF MONITORING THE GOVERNMENT PERFOMANCE. IF THEY GET EVIDENCE OF ANY WRONG ACTIVITYS OF RULING GOVERNMENT THEY SHOULD CONSIDER THAT AS A VIOLATION OF POWER AND TAKE REQUIRED ACTION.

FOR ELECTING PRECEDENT ONE THIRD OF THE VOTE SHOULD BE RESRVED FOR SENIOR MILITARY OFFICIALS, ONE THIRD TO MP'S AND REMAINING ONE THIRD TO MLA'S.

JUDISIORY SYSTEM SHOULD BE UNDER THE PRECIDENT OF THE NATION.

PRECEDENT SHOULD MAINTAIN A ADVICERY COMMITY WHICH INCLUDES SENIOR OFFICIALS OF THE MILITARY AND OTHER EXPERTS.

A SEPARATE GOVERMENT DEPARTMENT SHOULD BE AVAILABLE FOR ALL ELECTION PURPOSES UNDER PRECEDENT OF THE NATION.

MILITARY HIGHER OFFICIALS ALSO SELECTED THROUGH QUALIFIED PERSONS DRAW ELECTION.

THIS IS ONLY A BRIEF EXPLANATION; WE KNOW GOVERNMENT STRUCTURES ARE VERY HUGE AND HAVE LOT OF COMPLICATIONS IN DEMOCRACY SYSTEM.

NOW I WILL TELL SOMETHING ABOUT NATION'S INSIDE AND OUT SIDE PRACTICES. WE CAN CONSIDER WHOLE EARTH AS A VILLAGE AND OUR COUNTRY AS OUR HOME. WE KNOW EVERY HOME CONTAINS MORE THAN ONE PERSON. LIKEWISE INSIDE EVERY COUNTRY ALSO SEVERAL IDEOLOGIES, CULTURES AND ETHNICITIES. DIVERSITY AND DIFFERENCES ARE A COMMON ONE IT START FROM OUR NEXT PERSONS AND DID NOT END IN THE LAST PERSON. WE CAN NOT TELL TO ANYBODY THAT I WILL ACCEPT YOU ONLY WHEN YOU BECOME 100% LIKE ME. EVEN OUR CHILDRENS OR PARENTS NOT 100% LIKE US IN ALL MEANS HOW WE CAN SAY LIKE THAT. FOR A WELL BEING OF LIFE UNDER ANY COUNTRY EVERY ONE NEED THIS UNDERSTANDING.

AS PER MUSLIM SCHOLERS CLASSIFICATION ALL NATIONS COMES UNDER THREE CATEGORY.

NATIONS WITH NON-MUSLIM OR MUSLIM MEJORITY AND PRACTICING TRADITIONAL OR MODERN LAWS IN GOVERNMENT SYSTEM

MUSLIM MAJORITY NATIONS PRACTISING ISLAMIC LAW AND CULTURE IN THE GOVERNMENT SYSTEM.

NATIONS WHO TREATING MUSLIMS CITYSENS INSIDE THEIR NATION AS ENEMYS.

FIRST TWO CATEGORY OF NATIONS MATTER, NON-MUSLIM SOCIETYS AND MUSLIM SOCITYS LIVING UNDER THE UMBRELLAS OF MUTUAL UNDERSTANDING, PEACE AND HARMANY. IN THE THIRD CATOGORY NATIONS MATTER THAT IS A THRET FOR PEACE AND HARMANY OF ENTIRE MANKIND. SO, NATIONS PRACTICING GOOD HUMAN CULTURE AND TRADITIONS SHOULD INVOLVE IN THIS MATTERS FOR SOLUSION OF PROBLEM AND BETTERNESS OF THAT SOCITY. ESPECIALY SECOND CATEGORY ISLAMIC NATIONS.

NOW A DAYS ALSO KILAFATH IS POSSIBLE FOR MUSLIM NATIONS BY TRANSFORM ORGANIZATION OF MUSLIM CONTRYS(OIC) TYPE ORGANIZATIONS TO KILAFATH BY TRANSFER 50% OF EVERY MUSLIM NATIONS RULING POWER UNDER SUCH

ORGANIZATION AND MAKE THAT ORGANIZATION AS A UNIFICATION FACTOR FORTHE ENTIRE MUSLIM WORLD. CHANGE ORGANISATION STRUCTURE BY ASSINGING ISLAMIC GOVERNING BODYS AND SHURA COMMITYS THROUGH THE VOTING ELECTION AND DRAW ELECTION FROM THE QUALIFIED PERSONALITIESE FROM THE PARTICIPATING NATIONS.

I AM SURE, IF THIS KIND OF TRANSFORMATION WILL HAPPENDS, IT WILL HELP FOR THE BETTERNESS AND PROGRESS OF THE MUSLIM COMMUNITY AND THE ENTIRE WORLD.

CHAPTER-12

129

UNITED NATIONS

UNITED NATIONS UNITING US YET WE ARE UNDER DIFFERENT NATIONS. WE ALL NEED TO STRENTHEN UNITED NATIONS IN THE FUTURE ALSO. I HAVE SOME SUJECTIONS ESPECIALLY RELATED TO THE VITO POWER.

MY SUJECTION IS GIVE VITO POWER TROUGH ELECTION.

WE CAN CONDUCT ELECTION THROUGH POINT BASIS ELECTION SYSTEM. GIVE 1 POINT FOR EVERY ONE MILLION POPULATION OF A CONTRY. SUPPOSE A COUNTRY HAVE 250 MILLION POPULATION THEY WILL GET 250 POINTS. AFTER THIS SETUP WE CAN CONDUCT VITO ELECTION EVERY 5 YEAR FOR FIVE POSITIONS. INTERESTED CONTRYS HAVING MINIMUM ONE MILLION POPULATION CAN CONTEST IN THIS ELECTION.

I AM SURE IT WILL GIVE NEW LIFE AND ENERGY TO UNITED NATIONS. THAT WILL HELP THE BETTER FUTURE OF ALL HUMANS ON EARTH.

CHAPTER-13

SOCIALISM AND COMMUNISM

SOCIALISM IS NOT A BAD IDEA BUT IT IS NOT WELL IN ITS PURE FORM IN ALL MEANS. SOCIALISM ADVACATING EQUALITY IN ALL MEANING FOR SOCIETY LIFE. THE BETTER PART OF SOCIALISM IS EQUALITY OF HUMAN SOCIAL STATUS AS A HUMAN. AS PER ISLAM THIS IS ALSO TRUE.

FINANCIAL EQUALITY OF HUMAN BEING IS THE BAD PART OF SOCIALISM. SURVIVAL OF THE FITTEST IS THE LAW IMPLIMENTED IN NATURE BY GOD ALMIGHTY, BUT NOT THE WHOLE LAW OR DECISION OF GOD ALMIGHTYS IN ALL MEANS BUT MOST OF THE TIME GOD ALMIGHTY ALLOWS LAW OF NATURE THAT GOD ALMIGHTY CREATED FOR US.

I MEAN THAT EVERY LIVING AND NON LIVING THINGS CONTINOUES UNDER DIFFERENT NATURAL LAWS CREATED BY GOD. THE LAW OF ACHIEVEMENTS IN OUR LIFE IS EXPECT MORE AND PERFORM WELL.

ACCORDING TO ISLAM HEAR AFTER LIFE SUCCESS IS CONSIDER AS THE BIGEST ACHIEVEMENT. WHO WILL WIN HEAR AFTER WILL GET HEAVEN. WHO WILL REACH HEAVEN ALSO HAVE DIFFERENT STATUSUS ACCORDING TO THEIR GOOD DEEDS. SO GOD ALMIGHTY NOT ENTERTAINING EQUAL FACILITY STATUS EVEN IN HEAEVEN ALSO. THAT DID NOT MEANS THAT GOD ALMIGHTY STRICTLY STICK US ON ANY POSITION IN EARTHLY LIFE. IF YOU READ

DESTINY-QADHR CHAPTER OF THIS BOOK YOU WILL GET MUCH MORE UNDERSTANDING ABOUT THAT.

NOW I WILL COME TO THE POINT OF SOCIALISMS FINACIAL SIDE. AS PER MY OBSERVATION I WILL TELL SOME THING ABOUT SOCIALISM IMPLEMENTED CONTRY UUSR. MY OBSERVATION IS THE FAILURE OF UUSR SOCIAL SYSTEM DUE TO THE LESS PRODUCTIVITY OF THEIR PEOPLS. HOW IT HAPPENED MAIN REASON IS SOCIAL ECONOMICAL POLICIES OF THE GOVERNMENT.

AT THAT TIME THEY IMPLEMENT A WAGE RANGE SYSTEM ACTUALLY THAT IS AGAINST THE LAW OF NATURE OF HUMANS. DOCTORS, ENGINEERS AND HELPERS PROVIDED ALMOST SAME BASIC SALARY BECAUSE OF SOCIALIST POLICY. THIS POLICY MAKE DISAPPOINTED IN HIGHER QUALIFIED INDIVIDUALS. THIS ALSO DESCARAGE THE PEOPLES ATITUDE TO PURSURE HIGHER EDUCATION BECAUSE OF LESS BENEFIT COMPARED TO EFFORT. THEY STARTED TO THINK THAK IF OUR CHILDREN DID NOT STUDY MUCH MORE ALSO THEY WILL GET THE SAME SALARY RANGE AS DOCTORS AND ENGINIEERS GETTING. SO THE END RESULT IS PEOPLES BECOME LASY. THIS KIND OF ACTIONS AGAINST THE NATURAL FLOW OF HUMAM PROGRESS NOT BRINGING THE SOCCIETYS TO HIGHER

ACHIEVEMENTS ACCORDING TO THEIR EFFORT.

RESERVATION AND PENSION SYSTEMS ARE OTHER REASONABLY GOOD SIDE OF SOCIALIST ECONOMY. PENSION GENERALIZATION FOR EVERY BODY IS A BAD IDEA. ONLY PROVIDE PENSIONSION TO FINANCIALLY POOR PEOPLES AFTER ATTAINING PENSION AGE. UNEMPLOYMENT PENSION IS ALSO A BAD IDEA, INSTEAD THAT SPEND THAT MONEY FOR SOFT SKIL DEVELOPMENT AND JOB TRAINING. RESERATION SHOULD BE BASED ON REGION, FINANCE AND DISEBILITYS BUT NOT MORE THAN 30%.

COMMUNISM: COMMUNISM BELIVES IN THE SURVIVAL OF FITTEST THEORY LIKE CAPITALISM. BUT COMMUNIST PHYLOSOPHERS LIKE TO STAND WITH POOR AND LABOUR CLASSESS OF THE SOCIATY. FOR THE SURVIVAL OF SUCH PEOPLES BY BECOME FIT THEY MADE UNITENESS IN THAT CLASSESS OF THE SOCIETY THROUGH THEIR COMMUNIST ORGANIZATIONS. WE KNOW WHETHER LOW OR HIGH PSITION JOB MOST OF US ARE EMPLOYEES. SO AFTER GET GOVERNMENT FORMATION CHANCE COMMUNIST LEADERS CONCENTRATED ON THE OVERAL SYSTEM CHANGE FOR THE BENEFITS OF EMPLOYEE CLASS. AS PER MY UNDERSTANDING COMMUNISM IS MORE THAN A PARTY IT IS A IDEOLOGY AND

RELIGION BELIVES IN NATURAL LAWS. THEIR INTERPRETATION OF FINANCE IN SUCH WAY IS NOT SO REALISTIC. IF THEY PLANNED THEIR COMMUNIST ECONOMY AS BY MONITERING THE REAL SITUATIONS OF THE SOCIETY THEY MAY SUCCEDE LIKE CURRENT CHINESE ECONOMY.

CHAPTER-14

EARTH AND ENVIRONMENT

EVERYTHING NEAR OR ON EARTH INCLUDING OURSELVES WE CAN COLLECTIVELY CALLED EARTH AND ITS ENVIRONEMENT. SO IT IS VERY IMPORTANT TO US TO MAINTAIN OUR EARTH AND ENVIRONMENT SAFE AND SECURE. EVERYTHING IS MUTUALY LINKED IF A BIG CHANGE HAPENDS FROM ANY WHERE THE ENTAIRE SYSTEM WILL CHANGE. SUPPOSE IF SOME ANIMAL SPECIOUS IS DESAPEARING ENTERELY, THAT WILL MAKE A POSITIVE OR NEGATIVE CHANGE IN THE TOTAL SYSTEM. THIS KIND OF CHANGES EVEN RESULT IN CLIMET CHANGE, SOIL FERTILITY AND GROWTH OF PLANTS SAME AS IF THE ABOVE MENTIONED CLIMET, SOIL FERTILITY AND PLANTS LIFE CHANGES IT WILL AFFECT ECOSYSTEM AND EARTHLY LIFE ALSO. SO EVERYTHINGS EXISTENCE IS MUTUALY LINKED.

GOD ALMIGHTY IMPLEMENTED NATURAL LAWS EVERY WHERE IN GODS CREATION. THE UNIVERSE MOST OF THE THINGS CONTINOUVING UNDER DIFFERENT NATURAL LAWS, BUT PARTIALY EXEPT BY LIVING ORGANISMS, BECAUSE WE HAVE SOUL AND ITS INTERACTION ZONE MIND. LIVING ORGANISMS SOUL LEADING THEM THROUGH THEIR BODY AND MAKE THEM FREE IDENTITY. BUT OUR BODY ARE BUILT BY SMAL ELEMENTS WHICH ARE NORMALLY

FOLLOWING NATURAL LAWS UNDER OUR BODY PRE-PROGRAM.

THAT IS WHY LIVING ORGANISMS HAVE A UPPER HAND IN THIS UNIVERSE. IN THE CASE OF EARTHLY LIFE HUMANS ARE THE LEADER AMONGS ALL. ACCORDING TO QURAN ALLAH ALMIGHTY CALLING HUMANS AS THE KALIFA OF EARTH, NOT TO CALL A SINGLE PERSON ALLAH CALLED EVERY HUMAN AS KALIFA MEANS THE LEADER AMONGS ALL OTHER EARTHLY ENVIROMENT AND ECOSYSTEM. HUMANS LEADERS OR KALIFA IS THE LEADER OF HUMAN SOCIETYS THAT ARE OUR SOCIAL POSITIONS. WE KNOW MOST POWEFULL OR INFLUENCIAL PERSONS CAN DO MUCH MORE THAN NORMAL PERSONS. HUMANS POSITION IS KALIFA, THE LEADER POSITION, SO WE ARE THE MOST RESPONSIBLE PERSONS FOR MAINTAINING A GOOD BALANCED LIFE IN EARTH.

NOW I WILL TELL ABOUT OUR EXISTENCE THROUGH KNOWLEDGE. IF WE WILL FIND THE SECRET OF ANY NATURAL LAW OR PHENOMINA, WE CAN ALSO TRANSFORM THINGS AS PER THAT NATURAL LAW. GOD ALMIGHTY IS THE ONLY CREATER AND ALL POWER TRANSFORMER OF THE UNIVERSES. OUR ROLE IS NOT THE CREATOR. OUR ROLE IS THE TRANSFORMER ROLE. IF WE WANT TO TRANSFER ONE THING TO ANOTHER WE CAN

TRY AND LOT OF THINGS CAN MAKE POSSIBLE.

CREATION MEANS CREATE SOMETHING FROM NOTHING. THAT IS NOT POSSIBLE FOR US.

ONES WE UNDERSTAND THE SECRET OF RAINING WE CAN ALSO PARTICIPATE IN THE RAINING PROCESS. GOD ALMIGHTY HAVE NO OBJECTION FOR THAT, BUT DO FOR GOOD PURPOSE. LIKE WISE EVERYTHING IS ALLOWABLE THROUGH GOOD WAY FOR GOOD INTENSIONS.

SOME ONE WILL ARISE A QUISTION IF ALL THE BUILDING MATERIALS OF A LIVINNG CELL AND ORGANISM IS AVAILABLE IN EARTH IS IT POSSIBLE TO MAKE ONE? IF IT POSSIBLE YOU CAN MAKE IT THROUGH GOOD WAYS. ONE THING I CAN SURELY TELL, IF OUR CLONING OR CELL MAKING WITHOUT GOD ALMIGHTYS PERMISSION NO LIFE WILL EMERGES. WE MAY BUILD BODY BUT THE SOUL INSERTION IS WITH GOD ALMIGHTYS SIDE, IF GOD WISHES GOD WILL DO THAT.

WE KNOW HUMAN BABY WILL LIVE FROM THE BEGINNING EMBRIO STAGE WITH THEIR MOTHER SUPPORT, BUT THE BABY GETTING REAL INDIVITUAL IDENTITY AFTER SOME MONTHS OF THEIR STARTING. IN THAT STAGE SOUL WILL PLACE ON BABYS BODY, AFTER A GOOD SETTING WITH BODY AND SOUL HUMAN WILL BE ABLE FOR A NEW

LIFE. BEFORE THAT STAGE IF NORMAL DELIVERY HAPPENDS OR REMOVE LIFE SUPPORT THE BABY WILL NOT CONTINOUE THEIR LIFE. THIS IS BECAUSE SOUL IS OUR LIFE AND REAL IDENTITY. WHEN OUR BODY AND SOUL COMBINATION BECOME GOOD OUR MIND START TO DEVELOP, AT THAT TIME WE WILL GET OUR CONCIOUSNESS STATE. THIS WILL BEGINS FROM ONE YEAR.

SO ALL DEPENDS ON SOUL AND GETTING SOUL IS DEPENDS UP ON GOD ALMIGHTYS PERMISSION.

WE KNOW WE MADE SO MEANY ADVANCEMENT IN AGRICULTURE AND ANIMAL HUSBENDARY. OUR MOST OF THE CIVILISATIONS STARTED THROUGH AGRICULTURE SETTLEMENTS. PLANTING SINGLE PLANT SPECIES IN A WIDE AREA IS HUMAN STYLE OF AGRECULTURE FOR MASS PRODUCTION. NORNALLY ON EARTH WE CAN SEE A MIX UP OF ALL PLANTS AND TREES IN A AREA. OUR TYPE OF FARMING WILL ALSO CONTROLS THE CLIMET AND ENVIRONMENT IN NEGATIVE AND POSITIVE WAY. AS PER MY UNDERSTANDING EARTH HAVE SOUL, SITUATED INSIDE EARTHS BODY. SOIL, WATER AND STONES IN THE EARTHS BODY NOT CONTAINING EARTHS SOUL.

CHAPTER-15

SHERIATH AND ISLAMIC SOCIETY

SHERIATH IS THE LAW DERIVED FROM QURAN BY SCHOLERS AFTER THE DEATH OF PROPHET MUHAMMED. MEANS QURAN IS THE BASE OF SHERIATH BUT ALL THE LAWS AND OPINIONS OF SHERIATH IS NOT FROM QURAN.

AS PER MY UNDERSTANDING ABOVE 75% QURAN AYATHS(SENTENSES) ARE THE DIRECT WORDS OF ALLAH ALMIGHTY AND AROUND 20% ARE QUDUSI FROM ALLAH ALMIGHTY THROUGH THE WORDS OF PROPHET MUHAMMED, AROUND 3% ARE HUMAN MADE AYATHS. THE 3% HUMAN AYATHS ENTRY HAPPENED AT THE TIME OF QURAN KITAB(BOOK) COMBILATION AFTER PROPHET MUHAMMAD. WHAT ALLAH TOLD ALL ARE AVAIALABLE IN QURAN. OTHER THINGS ARE EXTRAS.

I WILL GIVE EXAMPLES SURAH FATHIHA IS A QUDHUSI ONE SURAH KAHF AND HADIDH ARE DIRECT ONES. SOME SURAH CONTAINING MIXED WORDS.

IN THE CASE OF HADIS KITHABS ALL CONTAINS MEANY FALLS AND NON-PROPHET HADHISES ALSO INCLUDING SAHIH MUSLIM AND BUHARI.

WE ARE CONSIDERING THESE TWO SOURCES ARE WITH QIYAS FOR SHARIATH PREPARATION. QURAN IS ALMOST FOUL PROOF, SO OUR CONCENTRATION OF RECHECKING SHOULD BE IN HADIDHS.

AFTER PROPHET MUHAMMED SO MEANY GENERATIONS PASSED NOW IT IS NOT POSSIBLE TO COLLECT HADIDHS DIRECTLY. SO WE SHOULD DEPENDS ON THESE HADIDH QITHABS WITH OUR SCIENTIFIC METHODOLOGY AND QURANIC KNOWLEDGE. IF ANY HADIDH CONTRADICT WITH QURAN WE CAN CONSIDER IT AS FALLS. IF ANY HADIDH CONTRADICT WITH PROVED SCIENTIFIC KNOWLEDGE WE CAN CONSIDER THAT HADIDH AS A FALLS ONE.

NO NEED TO FULLY DEPEND ON OLD INTERPRETATIONS. BECAUSE WE ARE THE GENERATION HAVE MORE COLLECTIVE KNOWLEDGE THAN SUCH GENERATIONS SCHOLERS.

IN THIS WAY CONSIDER QURAN AS THE SEED OF SHAREEATH AND TRUE LOGIC AND TRUE HADIDHS ARE THE WATER AND FERTILISER FOR FLURISHING THE TREE OF SHAREEATH AND ITS LIFESTYLE.

SHAREEATH OR QUARANIC LAW IS FOR HUMAN PURPOSE AND HUMANS ARE RESPOSIBLE FOR ITS IMPLIMENTATION.

HOW WE CAN INTERPRET IT, I WILL GIVE AN EXAMPLE. ACCORDING TO QURAN THE PANISHMENT FOR ROBERY IS HAND CUTTING. WE KNOW AT EARLY TIME HUMANS ARE MOSTLY EARN THEIR EARNINGS BY PHYSICAL JOBS. SO HAND IS IMPORTANT ORGAN FOR ROBERY. NOW A DAYS WE NEED TO EXTEND THIS SYSTEM TO

A NEXT LEVEL. THAT IS NO NEED TO CUT THE ROBERS HAND BUT BLOCK AL HIS ROBERY METHODS. WE KNOW SCAMS OF MILLION DOLLARS ARE HAPPENS AT SOME TIMES. SO BETTER METHOD IS USE THE INNER INTENSION OF QURANIC LAW AND GIVE HIM OR HER LONG PERIOD IMPRISENMENT AND BACK CHARGING.

ONLY THREE SITUATION ALLOWING CAPITAL PUNISHMENT

1) FOR MUDER OF A INNECENT PERSON
2) NON-MARRIAGE SEXUAL RELATION OF MEN AND WOMEN, EXTRAMARITAL SEXUAL RELATION, SAME GENDER SEX RELATIONS. ALL FOR ABOVE AGE 20
3) IN THE CASE OF ARMED ATTACKING AGAINST OUR NATION

NEXT FAMILY ASSET PARTITION, QURAN GIVES A BRIEF DISCRIPTION ABOUT ASSET PARTITION BUT THAT AYATHS ARE NOT DIRECT FROM ALLAH AND NOT THROUGH QUDHSI. IN THIS CASE WE CAN MAKE QIYAS OR ALLOW THE FAMILYS TO CHOOSE THEIR ON WAY.

ANOTHER IMPORTANT THING IS MARRIAGE AND MARRIAGE CONTRACT. QURAN IS LIMITING NUMBER OF MARRIAGE FOR WOMEN AT A TIME IS ONE AND MEN AT A TIME FOUR. IN THE MENS MARRIAGE CASE NATIONS HAVE THE RIGHT TO SET NUMER BTWEEN FOUR AND ONE IF REQUIRED. THAT

IS ALL BELONGS TO RULER OR KALIFAS DICISION WOMENS CASE NO CHANGE.

SOMEBODY WILL ASK ALLAH PERMITING THEN WHY CHANGING. THAT IS THE IMPORTANT OF A LEADER OR KALIFA IN ISLAM IT IS ALSO SOME TIMES BECOME A MATTER RELATED TO THE WELL BEING OF THE SOCIETY. AS PER NATIONS CONDITION HE CAN MAKE APROPRIATE DECISIONS BUT EVERYTHING SHOULD BE IN THE RANGE.

ISLAMIC MARRIAGE MEANS FORMAL CONTRACT BETWEEN TWO INDIVITUALS WITH THE GOVERNMENT ADMINISTRATION AND WITH WITNESS. MY RECOMENTATION IS THE CONTRACT SHOULD BE SINED BETWEEN WOMEN AND MEN WITH TWO WITNESS FROM WOMENS FAMILY AND TWO WITNESS FROM MENS FAMILY. THE GOVERNING BODY SHOULD BE GOVERNMENT OF THAT NATION. FINANCIAL OR ASSET TRANSACTIONS LIKE MEHER OR ANY THING IS NOT REQUIRED

AFTER MARRIAGE CONTRACT MINIMUN THREE MONTH IS REQUIRED TO INVALIDATE THE CONTRACT IF BOTH OF THEM OR ONE REQUIRED. AFTER MARRIAGE CONTRACT INVALIDATION NEXT THREE MONTHS MARRIAGE IS NOT POSSIBLE FOR BOTH OF THEM WITH ANOTHER INDIVITUALS. IF THE COUPLE WANT TO REMARRIAGE WITH IN THAT TIME THEY CAN MARRY WITHOUT ANOTHER PERSONS ENTRY IN THEIR LIFE.

AFTER THAT ALSO THEY CAN REMARRY IF NOT ENGAGED WITH ANOTHER MARRIAGE. AFTER THREE MONTHS OF MARRIAGE INVALIDATION BOTH OF THEM CAN MARRY ANY OTHER PERSON AS FROM ISLAM ALLOWING STATUS PERSONS. A WRITTEN MARRIGE CONTRACT WILL NEVER BECOME INVALIDATED WITH ORAL COMENT OR INFORMAL INVALIDATION.

IF A MARRIAGE CONTRACT INVALIDATED AND COUPLES HAVE CHILDRENS, UP TO AGE 25 THE FATHER IS RESPONSIBLE FOR CHILDS EXPENSES, IF THE MOTHER OR CHILDREN WANTS.

I BEFORE EXPLAINED HUMANS ESPECIALY MUSLIM HUMANS ARE RESPOSIBLE FOR THE IMPLEMENTATION OF SHERIATH IN THEIR LIFE AND THEIR SOCIETYS. SOME PART OF SHERIATH WE CAN PRACTICE WITHOUT A GOVERNMENT.

COMPLETE IMPLEMENTATION IS ONLY POSSIBLE WHEN A SOCIETY OR GOVERNMENT RUN BY MUSLIMS OR NON-MUSLIMS INTERESTED IN IT AND MAKE IT AS THE LAW OF THEIR NATION.

I WILL GIVE AN EXAMPLE OF IT, ZAKATH (ASSET PURIFICATION TAX) SYSTEM IMPLIMENTATION IS COMPLETELY POSSIBLE ONLY THROGH A GOVERNMENT BODY. CRIMINAL PAMISHMENT SYSTEM OF SHERIATH STYLE IS ONLY POSSIBLE AND PRACTICABLE THROUGH A GOVERNMENT

SYSTEM. IT IS NOT PERMISIBLE TO INDIVITUAL TO PANISH ANOTHER PERSON THROUGH SHARIATH LAW IF A GOVERNMENT IS AVAILABLE THEIR.

SO A FORMAL GOVERNMENT SYSTEM IS REQUIRED FOR THE COMPLETE IMPLEMENTATION SYSTEM. WE KNOW AT THE TIME OF PROPHET MUHAMMED, PROPHET LEAD THE NATION. AFTER THAT FOUR KALIFAS CONTINOUE PROPHETS MISSION. LATER CHANGED THE RULING STRUCTURE TO A KING FAMILY RULING SYSTEM.

AS PER MY UNDERSTANDING PROPHET SHOW THE PATH AND DIRECTION AND HE SUCCEDED ALMOST 70% IN ITS IMPLIMENTATION AT HIS TIME. I WILL GIVE AN EXAMPLE, PROPHIT MUHAMMED PROMOTE SLAVE RELEASING AND PROPHET DONE BY HIS ACTION ALSO BUT PROPHET DID NOT SUCCEDED IN 100% RELEASING OF HIS TIMES SLAVES. MUSLIM UMMA(SOCIETY) TAKEN MEANY CENTURYS FOR ACHIVING THIS TASK IN THEIR CONTROLED AREAS. SUCH A WAY KILAFATH IS THE BEGINNING MODEL AND DIRECTION TO MODERN DEMOCRACY. BUT AFTER SOME YEARS OF PROPHETS DEATH MUSLIM UMMA (SOCIETY) RETURN BACK TO KING FAMILY RULE OF OLD STYLE.THEY DID NOT PROGRESED IN THE DIRECTION PROPHET SHOWNED.

SO A GOOD ADMINISTRATION AND LEADING SYSTEM IS REQUIRED FOR THE IMPLEMENTATION AND PROMOTION OF SHARIATH LAW IN HUMAN LIFE.

CHAPTER-16

WHO IS MORE IMPORTANT INDIVITUAL OR SOCIETY

ACTUALLY BOTH ARE SAME THING, AT THE SAME TIME DIFFERENT IMPORTANT IDENTITYS. INDIVIDUAL ARE THE SMALL UNDIVIDABLE UNITS OF THE SOCITYS. IN ANOTHER WORD WE CAN SAY SOCITY IS THE GROUP OF DIFFERENT INDIVIDUALS EXEPT THE SPECIFIC INDIVIDUAL OR OUR SELF IN OUR MATTER AND EXCLUDING OTHER INDIVIDUAL WHEN THEIR MATTER.

SO IT IS ECCENTIAL TO CONSIDER A SOCIETY FROM ITS INDIVIDUALS IDENTITY WHEN MAKING LAWS AND TREATING THEM UNDER THE LAWS.

IF WE ALLOWS ENTIRE RIGHT OR POWER TO SOCIETY OVER INDIVIDUALS IN EVERY MATTER IT WILL MAKE BIG PROBLEMS IN THAT SOCIETY AND INDIVIDUAL LIFE. IF WE GIVE ALL RIGHT TO INDIVIDUALS TO LIVE AS THEY WISHES THAT WILL ALSO MAKE PROBLEMS IN OTHER INDIVIDUALS LIFE AND IN THE SOCIETY.

SO A BALANCED PROPORTION OF RIGHTS BETWEEN BOTH IDENTITYS IS ESSENTIAL REQUIREMENT WHEN PREPARING AND APPLYING THE LAW.

THE RIGHTS SHOULD BE DOCUMENTED AS LAW AND IMPLIMENT THROUGH ITS ADMINISTRATIVE SYSTEM.

SO FUNDAMENTAL RIGHTS SHOULD BE IMPLEMENT FOR THE INDIVIDUALS AND RIGHTS OF POWER SHOULD BE GIVEN TO THE GOVERNMENT OF THE SOCIETY. BOTH

INDIVIDUALS FUNDAMENTAL RIGHTS AND SOCIETY LEADING GOVERMENTS RIGHTS OF POWER SHOULD BE DEVELOPE UNDER THE GREAT TRADITIONS AND VALUES OF MAN KIND WITH GREAT PRACTICAL WISDOM AND SCIENTIFIC THINKING.

THE AUTHORITYS SHOULD ENSURE THE USEFULLNESS OF EXISTING LAWS BY GREAT UPDATIONS OR GREAT INTERPRETATIONS. IN DEMOCRATIC SYSTEM PEOPLES CAN ALSO POSSIBLE TO INVOLVE INDIRECTLY IN THE LAW MAKING, IMPLIMENTING AND UP GRADATION BY THEIR SOCIAL ACTIVITIESE AND PARTICIPATE IN THE ELECTION.

CHAPTER-17

CONCLUSION

FROM MY LIFE UNDERSTANDING ONE OF THE GREAT THING I UNDERSTANDED IS, MATTERS ARE ACTUALLY LESS BUT ITS IMPLEMENTATION MAKES THE DIFFERENCE. I WILL GIVE SOME EXAMPLES

IF I WILL TELL TO PRACTICE THE TRUTH EVERY TIME OR BECOME A GOOD BUSINESS MAN OR PRACTICE VIRTUE EVERY TIME, EXERCISE EVERY DAY, WE WILL NOT FEEL AS MUCH DIFFICULTY IN A AVERAGE UNDERSTANDING. SO THESE ARE SMALL SENTENSES BUT IF YOU TAKE IT AS SERIOUS MATTER THEN YOU WILL UNDERSTAND ITS DIFFICULTIESE, BENEFITS AND REAL IMPORTANCE.

ONE OF THE GREAT QUALITY I OBSERVED IN GANDIJI IS GANDHIS AHIMSA POLICY (NON-KILLING OR NON-VIOLENCE). IN HIS LIFE, SO MEANY TIMES HE FACED DIFFICULTIESE FROM THE EXTERNAL WORLD IN THE AHIMSA PRACTICING AND TEACHING. BUT WITH DIFFICULTIESE GANDHI CONTINOUE HIS LIFE AND TEACHING OF AHIMSA AND HE ALMOST SUCCEDED IN THIS TEACHING AND PRACTICE. I AM TELLING THAT AHIMSA IS A SMALL WORD BUT IF YOU WANT TO IMPLIMENT IT IN YOUR LIFE AND TEACH IT TO THE SOCIETY YOU WILL FACE SOME TROUBLES AND DIFFICULTIESE IN THAT PATH OTHER THAN NORMAL LIFE. IF YOU SUCCEDED IN IT YOU ARE A REAL WINNER.

EVERY INDIVIDUALS SHOULD PRACTICE AHIMSA MINIMUM WITH HUMAN SOCIETY, ONLY GOVERNMENT OF THE NATION HAVE THE RIGHT TO GIVE CAPITAL PANISHMENT TO A HUMAN, ONLY IN THE CASE OF HE OR SHE DID A SERIOUS CRIME.

IF WE WANT SOMETHING VERY EXTREAMLY AND WE WORK FOR SUCH AMBITIONS THE CHANCE OF SUCCEED IN THAT WILL INCREASES, SOMEBODY CALLED IT AS LAW OF ATTRACTION I WOULD LIKE TO CALL IT AS LAW OF ATTRACTED FOCUSING AND APPROPRIATE ACTION.

FOCUS IS MOSTLY BASED ON ATTRACTION. IF WE FOCUSED ON SOMETHING OUR MIND AND SOUL WILL SPEND SOME MORE TIME FOR THAT. BECAUSE THAT MATTER IS FEEDED TO OUR SOULS FOCUS. EACH PERSONS BODY AND SOUL HAVE ITS ON DESIRES AND FOCUS ALSO. WE CAN CONTROLED AND FLURISH IT THROUGH OUR MIND AND SOUL. THEN OUR MIND AND SOUL STARTED TO CHASE THE FOCUSED THING.FROM THAT POINT WE WILL SEE MORE SUCH FOCUS RELATED THINGS IN OUR SURROUNDINGS, NOT BECAUSE OF SUCH THINGS REAL INCRESING IN THE SURROUNDINGS BEAUSE OF OUR FOCUSE ON THAT SUBJECT. WITH THIS KIND OF FOCUSE OUR MIND AND SOUL WILL EVERY TIME AWARE ABOUT OUR TASK THAT LEAD US TO SELECTION OF APROPRIATE TASK

ACHIEVING METHODS CONCIOUSLY OR UNCONCIOUSLY. OUR SIDE ACTIONS ON FOCUSED SUBJECT IS VERY IMPOETANT, BECAUSE IT IS NOT A COMPLETE AUTOMATIC SYSTEM. THAT IS NOW A DAYS SOME LAW OF ATTRACTIESE LACKING.

AMBITIONS ARE ALL WAYS ARISES IN OUR MIND, GOOD AMBITIONS ARE GOOD THINGS BUT ONLY TRY TO ACHIEVE IT THROUGH GOOD PATH. ACHIEVING ANY THING THROUGH BAD OR WRONG WAYS ARE AGAINST VIRTUES OF MANKIND. IF OUR AMBITION IS ALSO BAD OR WRONG DO NOT GO IN SUCH A WAY EAVEN THROUGH GOOD PATH.

BUILD YOUR PERSONALITY LIKE A MACHINE AND YOUR ACTIONS LIKE TOOLS INTERACTION. WITH OUT A GOOD MACHINE ITS TOOL IS EFFECTLESS. WE KNOWS THROWING BULLETS WITHOUT A GOOD GUN IS USELESS.

GOD ALMIGHTY LOVES ALL OF US, GOD INSISTING US TO LOVE OUR HUMAN FAMILY AS WELL AS THE WHOLE NATURE. GOD INSISTING US TO SUBMITING OUR WILL TO OUR PURPOSE OF LIFE MEAS GETTING GOD ALMIGHTYS ISHQ (LOVE) AND NEARNESS...